Everyday Handbooks

RELIGION IN THE UNITED STATES

Benson Y. Landis

NEW YORK

BARNES & NOBLE, INC.

PUBLISHERS • BOOKSELLERS • SINCE 1873

Library of Congress Catalogue Card Number: 65–14270

This is an original Everyday Handbook (Number 294). It was written by a distinguished author, carefully edited, and produced in accordance with the highest standards of publishing. The text was set on the Linotype in Times Roman by Hamilton Printing Company (Rensselaer, N.Y.). The paper for this edition was manufactured by the S. D. Warren Company (Boston, Mass.) and supplied by the Canfield Paper Company (New York, N.Y.). This edition was printed by Hamilton Printing Company and bound by Sendor Bindery (New York, N.Y.). The cover was designed by Rod Lopez-Fabrega.

TABLE OF CONTENTS

PART ONE: DESCRIPTIONS OF CONTEMPORARY RELIGIOUS BODIES (Continued)

PART TWO: QUICK-REFERENCE GUIDE 77

PART THREE: GLOSSARY OF RELIGIOUS TERMS .. 93

PREFACE

This book presents an introduction to origins, doctrines, forms of worship, and organizations of religious bodies in the United States. It emphasizes many of the distinctive experiences of the people of this nation in their institutions of religion, and offers opportunity for comparisons among them.

Part One includes brief descriptions of the main groups or families of religious bodies and of the principal denominations, alphabetically arranged. Attention is also given to the religions of the American Indians and to a few informal fellowships not known as denominations, such as Alcoholics Anonymous and the Oxford Group.

Part Two is a Quick-Reference Guide, also alphabetical, to matters of general concern to the numerous American religious organizations. Here many common interests, beliefs, and positions are noted. Summaries are included of such topics as "ecumenical" movements (those for co-operation and unity); the principle of the separation of church and state; the trend from a predominantly Protestant society to one of four main religions—Protestantism, Roman Catholicism, Judaism, and Eastern Orthodoxy; the development of social activities in most churches; the resolutions and pronouncements of the various denominations on public issues; the historic and continuing interest of religious bodies in education; the current building boom; and the periodic occurrence of large mass revivals and of smaller revivals that have resulted in new denominations.

Part Three consists of an alphabetical Glossary of frequently used religious terms.

Part Four contains summaries of religious statistics. The main sources for these statistics are the publications of religious bodies; the Censuses of Religious Bodies published by the Bureau of the Census; and the yearly reports made by practically all of some 250 religious bodies to the *Yearbook of American Churches,* published by the National Council of Churches.

While the works of many scholars were carefully studied by the author during the preparation of this volume, the book is intended for a general audience, including both students and lay persons. Hence technicalities which may be important to theologians and other scholars are of necessity omitted, and an effort has been made to define and explain clearly a number of difficult or unfamiliar terms in the subjects discussed.

Finally, the author recognizes that there is "unorganized religion" in the United States, that many persons professing a religion or a religious preference are not found listed on the membership rolls of institutions. There is, however, no adequate way of documenting or describing their interests and activities.

BENSON Y. LANDIS

PART ONE

DESCRIPTIONS OF CONTEMPORARY RELIGIOUS BODIES

The descriptions in this section deal mainly with the largest denominations and groups of denominations in the United States. With very few exceptions (such as the Christian and Missionary Alliance, the Ethical Culture group, and the Moravians), independent religious groups with a membership of fewer than 100,000 are not included. Since the arrangement is alphabetical, the reader can easily find pertinent information about any of the major denominations. In addition, a few entries relate to certain religious groups of special interest, such as, for example, the American Indians, a number of so-called "small sects," well-known informal fellowships, and independent local churches.

For each denomination, information on its history, main doctrines, form of worship, and mode of organization or government is presented. The information was obtained chiefly from the following sources: Censuses of Religious Bodies; recent publications of the several denominations themselves; and reports by church officials to the *Yearbook of American Churches,* a compilation of data from all faiths published by the National Council of Churches.

(For statistics on the various groups discussed in this section, see "Summary of Statistics," p. 102.)

ADVENTISTS

The Adventists are a group of religious bodies which emphasize particularly their special belief in the anticipated physical return of Jesus Christ to earth. This doctrine has of course been taught to Christians ever since the days of the early Apostolic Church; Paul's Epistles frequently refer to his belief in the Second Coming. From 1825 to 1845 the doctrine had extraordinary repercussions, for during that period many students of the Bible in North America and in Europe caused a great stir among the masses by predicting that the Second Coming was at hand. Wealthy people and those of the highest rank were among those committed to this belief, which became the occasion for a sort of religious renaissance. And to this day the Adventists and a number of other religious groups adhere to the same doctrine.

By 1840 many Christians in the United States had been attracted to "second advent evangelism." Among prominent leaders were the Reverend Joshua V. Hines, of Boston, and William Miller, the latter achieving eminence both as a military expert (he was once a captain in the Federal Army) and as a Baptist minister. Their followers included a group of a few pioneers who met in Washington, New Hampshire, in 1844 to affirm their unshakable belief in the imminent personal advent of Christ and began to observe Saturday as the Sabbath.

According to William Miller, not only was the time of the Advent at hand, but, in fact, the day could be definitely fixed in advance. He announced confidently that Jesus Christ would return during the year from March 21, 1843 to March 21, 1844. When the predicted event failed to take place, Miller proclaimed that he had made an error in his calculations. Nevertheless, by 1845 about a thousand local churches in the United States, some belonging to well-known denominations, had become "Adventist." Some of them convened in a general conference at Albany, New York. Finally, in 1860, a number of these local churches set up a central headquarters and a publishing office and formally adopted the name of Seventh Day Adventists.

There are now five Adventist bodies in the United States, the largest of which is the Seventh Day Adventists.

Doctrines. The Holy Scriptures are the rule governing faith and practice. The Godhead is a trinity: the eternal Father; the Son of the Father; and the Holy Spirit. Baptism is by immersion. Eternal life comes to the redeemed as a free gift based on their belief in Christ. On the Second Coming, the "mortal shall put on immortality." The Second Coming is the hope of the Church. Strict attention must be given to "signs of the times." No man can really know the year or the hour of the Second Coming, but prophecy can reveal cues about them to discerning persons. Meanwhile the ministry of Christ goes on within heaven, so that God's judgment decides all issues between the just and the unjust.

ellen white - prophet 7 day advocant

Seventh Day Adventists are expected to refrain from the use of intoxicating beverages, tobacco, and narcotics. Many Adventists are also vegetarians. Numerous publications of the denomination teach the essentials of healthful living.

Members are required to support the Church by payment of tithes, calculated on the scriptural basis of one-tenth of his income from each member. The gospel work includes the administration of hospitals both in the United States and abroad and the sponsorship of evangelistic missions in many lands.

Worship. The worship is informal, consisting of hymns, reading of the Scriptures, prayers, sermons, and offerings, as determined by each pastor and his congregation.

Organization. The local church has a large measure of autonomy in its business affairs, but it must belong to a conference which has broad powers of supervision. The conference pays the minister's salary.

Advent Christian Church. Of the four other Adventist bodies, the Advent Christian Church is the largest. This body was organized in 1855 under the leadership of Jonathan Cummings, who founded the separatist group because he believed in a different interpretation of the Biblical teaching on eternal life. Local churches are congregational in government. A district conference ordains the ministers. Missions have been set up abroad to supplement those in the United States.

BAHÁ'Í

The Bahá'í faith developed from a religious movement that originated in Persia in 1844. Its followers regard it as a universal religion, that is, one teaching the unity of all religions. Branches have been organized in most of the nations of the world. (Ironically, the adherents of Bahá'í were expelled in 1960 from the land of its origin, modern Iran.)

A religious movement known as Babism was founded in Islam in 1844–45 by Mirza Ali Muhammad, who assumed the title of Bab, meaning "Door" or "Gate." (He was executed by Muslims in 1850.) One of his disciples was Mirza Husayn Ali (1870–92), given the title of Baha'ullah, which means "Glory of God." At the beginning, the Baha led a reform movement within Islam, but he subsequently added elements of Christianity and other religions. He is regarded as the founder of Bahá'í. He was exiled from Bagdad in 1852.

Doctrines. The principal tenets emphasize the essential oneness of mankind, the affirmation that spiritual power has been given to human beings so that they may fulfil their desire for unity. The following excerpt from the teachings of the founder is most often quoted: "Unfettered search after truth and the abandonment of all superstition and prejudice; the oneness of mankind—all are 'leaves of one tree, flowers in one garden'; religion must be a cause of love and harmony, else it is no religion; all religions are one in their fundamental principles; religion must conform with science, bringing faith and reason into full accord; and recognition of the unity of God and obedience to His commands are revealed through His devine manifestations."

Worship. Bahá'í has no professional clergy. Believers and inquirers meet in small groups to study "revealed words." Instruction must always be made available without compensation.

Organization. A local assembly of the faith consists of nine persons. (The number *nine* is regarded as a symbol of perfection.) To apply for voting membership in an assembly, one must be twenty-one years old and a resident of the community in which the group meets. Each application must be approved by the assembly after examination of the applicant's qualifications. The several local assemblies elect nine persons who make up the governing board of the National Spiritual Assembly.

BAPTISTS

A number of Baptist churches were organized in Europe during the fifteenth century. Early in the sixteenth century, a group of rebaptizers, the Anabaptists, made independent witness to their faith in Switzerland and Germany. The Anabaptists held that persons baptized in infancy must on reaching maturity profess their faith and be baptized again in order to secure admission to full church membership. They encountered stern opposition from both Protestants and Roman Catholics but steadily increased in number despite persecution. Many were driven to the Low Countries, where they were shepherded by Menno Simons (see Mennonites). From Holland the influence of the Anabaptists and of the Mennonites spread to England, resulting in the formation of Baptist churches there. The Confession of Faith published by these churches in 1644 proclaimed baptism by immersion as the form approved by the Apostolic Church.

The first Baptist churches in Colonial America were the ones organized by John Clarke at Newport (Rhode Island) in 1638 and another established by Roger Williams at Providence in 1639. Williams, who founded Providence and soon thereafter became the most prominent apostle of religious liberty in the New World, had been banished from Massachusetts in 1635 for having, in the words of the indictment, "broached and divulged new and dangerous opinions against the authority of magistrates." In Providence he taught the basic principles of the Baptist faith to a small group of adherents. Williams baptized Ezekiel Holliman, who in turn baptized Williams, who then baptized ten others. Thus the second earliest congregation came into being. Apparently, John Clarke, who had come from New Hampshire to found Newport and to establish a Baptist church there, was unaware of the work of Williams, nor did the latter know about Clarke's endeavors.

The numerous Baptist denominations today constitute the largest family of Protestant denominations in the United States. At various times, divisions within this large group have occurred; for example, in Newport, site of the earliest church, a Seventh Day Baptist Church was founded in 1671. The Baptists include Calvinists (see Presbyterians) as well as many very active groups of non-Calvinists. A rigid Calvinism prevailed among the pioneering Baptists in the Appalachian region and elsewhere in the South, where the Primitive Baptists organized to oppose the activities of missionaries sent there from abroad. Those who defended the missionaries were popularly known as "Missionary Baptists." In 1845 the slavery issue impelled several associations of Baptist churches to form the Southern Baptist Convention, seceding from a Baptist missionary organization with headquarters in Boston, Massachusetts. (The Southern Baptist Convention today has members in all parts of the country.) The Northern Baptist Convention was organized in 1907 and was renamed the American Baptist Convention in 1950. A Negro Baptist church was organized as early as

1788, and today two of the three largest Baptist bodies are predominantly Negro: the National Baptist Convention, U.S.A., Inc., and the National Baptist Convention of America.

Doctrines. Compared to those of other religious groups, the doctrinal requirements for membership in Baptist churches are minimal. Baptists acknowledge no human founder of their church, accept no human authority, subscribe to no human creed. The New Testament is their sole authority. Confessions of faith have been prepared by various assemblies but are not binding upon local churches. Always ready to defend freedom of conscience in religion and worship, Baptists oppose any form of regimentation of their members in spiritual matters. They observe baptism and the Lord's Supper but regard them as ordinances rather than sacraments. They believe in the validity and inspirational character of the Scriptures, the Lordship of Jesus Christ, the immortality of the soul, the brotherhood of man, the need for redemption from sin, and the ultimate triumph of the Kingdom of God.

Although baptism by immersion is the usual practice, local churches are not required to use this method. In fact, some accept applicants by letter of transfer from other churches even though these members may have been baptized by the pouring of water instead of by immersion. Some "dedicate" infants in a special ceremony of this kind, baptizing them again, mostly by immersion, when they become full members of their church. (Note that baptism by immersion is also practiced by religious bodies other than the Baptists: e.g., the Churches of Christ, the Christian Churches, or Disciples of Christ, and the numerous Brethren and Mennonite bodies. Many religious organizations permit baptism by immersion if the individual prefers this method to pouring. The Eastern Churches immerse infants as well as adults.)

Worship. The form of worship is controlled by the local congregation. On the whole, Baptist worship is in the general Protestant or Evangelical tradition: hymns, reading of the Scriptures, prayers, sermons, and offerings, the sequence being determined by the local church and minister.

Organization. Baptist bodies are strictly congregational in government. The local churches may ordain persons of their choice to the ministry. District, state, and national conventions are held for the advancement of common interests, such as home and foreign missions, education, social welfare, and relief activities abroad.

Nevertheless, the resolutions passed at these conventions are not binding upon local churches, which are free to accept, reject, or ignore them as they please.

BRETHREN CHURCHES

Three groups of religious bodies are known as Brethren Churches: the German Baptist Brethren, the River Brethren, and the Plymouth Brethren.

German Baptist Brethren. In 1719 Peter Becker, leader of a Pietistic group of Brethren in Europe, migrated to the United States (Germantown, Pennsylvania) with a small company of his followers. In 1720 Alexander Mack crossed the Atlantic together with fifty-nine families (a total of 126 persons). Thus the nucleus of a religious movement was transferred from the Old World to the New. (The original adherents who remained in Europe have been lost to history.)

The new religious communities arising in Germany at the end of the seventeenth century were not organized by Protestants as opponents of Catholicism but rather by certain Protestants (the German Pietists) discontented with the barrenness and dogmatics of early Protestantism. They emphasized the individual's inner life instead of creed or ritual.

Among their prominent leaders were Philip Jacob Spener and August Herman Francke (founder of the University of Halle), who conducted a mission and a trade school in Halle and organized the famous orphanage there. They studied the Bible intensively, reviewed church history, and advocated moderation in theological thought. Two of their devout students, Ernest Hochman and Alexander Mack, founded a community at Schwarzenau, Westphalia, on the Eider River. In 1708 Alexander Mack and seven companies went down to the riverbank and chose one of their number by lot to baptize Alexander Mack by immersing him in the river three times in the name of the Father, the Son, and the Holy Ghost (possibly the first Protestant trine immersion). Then Alexander Mack similarly baptized the others, and they established the first congregation of a church that was separate from Catholicism and from the Protestantism of the time. Because of their method of baptism, they became known as the "Dunkers" (German, Täufer) or German Baptists. Their group was also known as Church of the Brethren.

The Brethren, ignoring questions of dogma, such as "Apostolic Succession," wrote no creed. They soon worked out for themselves an authentic church life comparable to that of the Mennonites and Friends (but they had no contacts with these other religious groups). The beginnings at Schwarzenau led to formation of congregations in Switzerland and in the German Palatinate. Peter Becker and Alexander Mack, members of these German congregations, migrated to set up the Church of the Brethren in America, where they were called "Dunkers" as in Europe.

Their experiences paralleled those of other colonial religious bodies; as they spread westward and gained adherents, diverging ideas led to separatist movements. One of the first breaks from the parent body was that of Johann Conrad Beissel and his followers, who left to establish a monastic community at Ephrata, Pennsylvania. (This community no longer exists, but its buildings have been preserved and are open to the public.)

The Church of the Brethren, the largest of five German Baptist bodies, is orthodox trinitarian. The communion service, celebrated at evening, is preceded by the ceremony of the washing of feet. The seriously ill are anointed. Nonresistance is taught and many of the members refuse to bear arms in time of war. Members also "testify" against the use of alcoholic beverages. The Church carries on extensive missions abroad for purposes of education and relief. The mode of worship is altogether informal and locally determined. The form of church government is a modification of the presbyterian system (see Presbyterians).

The River Brethren. This is a popular term that may have been derived either from an organization called "Brotherhood Down the River" (active in Lancaster County, Pennsylvania) or from the custom of baptizing members in a river. The first River Brethren, comprising a small group of settlers who came from Basle, Switzerland, to western Lancaster County in 1751, were generally considered to be Mennonites. Numerous revivals were conducted in the region about 1770, and Jacob Engle was the first minister chosen. The original group soon broke up into various segments, and today the organization consists of three small bodies practicing immersion and nonresistance. The River Brethren are orthodox trinitarian, with a major interest and activity in foreign missions. Their worship is informal. Two of the three bodies have bishops as administrators, adhering to a modified episcopal form of organization.

The Plymouth Brethren. This religious body originated in England and Ireland in the 1820's. One of the early associations was founded at Plymouth, England, whence the name Plymouth Brethren. Among the notable leaders was John Nelson Darby, who subsequently established congregations in the United States and elsewhere. This body of Christians considers the various denominators of the world to be unscriptural; hence it does not co-operate with other religious bodies. There are eight branches in the United States.

The Plymouth Brethren accept the general Evangelical teachings on the Trinity, the absolute deity of Christ, atonement for man by Christ's sacrificial death, and the literal interpretation of the Bible. They do not have a paid or professional ministry and, since they own no church buildings, meet for informal worship in homes and rented halls. The organizational procedures of these small groups are also very informal.

BUDDHISTS

Most Buddhists in the United States are persons born in the Orient or their descendants, living in the western United States and Hawaii. Those residing on the mainland refer to their organization as "Buddhist Churches."

The Buddhist religion originated in the sixth century B.C. in India, where there now are relatively few believers. Buddhism was founded as a reform movement within Hinduism by Prince Siddhartha Gautama (the Buddha). Deeply affected by the sufferings of the common people, he meditated on their condition and on the meaning of life. He renounced his royal rights and traveled on foot throughout the land for seven years, conversing with all sorts of people. He lived an ascetic life and devoted himself to meditation, beginning his new way of life by teaching five ascetic companions near Benares.

After Buddha's death, Buddhism divided into two branches: Hinayana, which remained close to the original simple teachings, and Mahayana, which expanded them to encompass popular beliefs in numerous divine beings, ritual and magic, and an afterlife with rewards and punishments. There are large numbers of Buddhists in Burma, Ceylon, Thailand, Vietnam, Laos, Korea, Japan, China, and the eastern parts of the Soviet Union. Buddhist temples in China and southeast Asia are beautiful edifices, perhaps reflecting the enthusiastic devotion of multitudes of adherents. In China many Buddhists are Confucianists as well, while in Japan many Buddhists are also Shintoists.

Doctrines. Buddha did not teach a personal deity; he taught that Nirvana, attainment of a state of passionlessness, without any flame of selfish desire, should be the universal goal. To the non-Buddhists who regard this doctrine as somewhat negative, the devout Buddhist replies that the true conception of his faith is definitely positive. Buddhism is said to be akin to the teaching of other religions that the self must be denied in order that true life will thus be attained. This doctrine does not suggest a state of unconsciousness or of indifference, but signifies a way of eventually achieving in Nirvana a freedom from self in a state of "perfect peace, goodness, and wisdom." Its believers are urged to avoid sensuality as well as excessive austerity.

Buddhists teach the Wheel of the Excellent Law, whose hub is truth, whose tire is wisdom, and whose spokes are true and good conduct. There are "Four Noble Truths": suffering; the origin of suffering; the passing away of the suffering; and the way that leads to the passing away of suffering. The way is an "Eightfold Path": right views; right aspirations; right speech; right conduct; right mode of livelihood; right endeavor; right mindfulness; and right meditation.

Worship and Organization. Worship is conducted by priests in the temples. In the United States the temples usually are not separate structures, but merely a number of rented rooms in buildings shared with other tenants. Meditation is an important method of worship as well as an effective aid in living the good life. The organization of temple worship is very simple. There is evidence of a renaissance of Buddhism in the nations of the Orient with the exception of mainland China. One aspect of this renaissance was indicated by the convocation of the Sixth Great Council of Buddhism, attended by laymen, priests, and monks, in Rangoon, Burma, in 1954–56, for re-examining the teachings of the religion.

The Council was convoked on the initiative of the Burmese Parliament to consider new measures for developing the spiritual and moral well-being of man.

CATHOLICS

(See OLD CATHOLICS; POLISH NATIONAL CATHOLICS; ROMAN CATHOLICS)

CHRISTIAN AND MISSIONARY ALLIANCE

This religious body was organized in New York City in 1881 by the Reverend A. B. Simpson, a Presbyterian clergyman. Mr. Simpson left the Presbytery of New York City at that time to conduct evangelistic work among the unchurched of the city, holding winter meetings in theaters and halls and summer meetings in a tent. Soon an independent congregation, the Gospel Tabernacle, was organized in New York, and evangelistic meetings were also held in other cities of the East. In 1887 two societies were formed, one for home missions, the other for evangelism overseas. The two were subsequently united into the Christian and Missionary Alliance, the present denomination.

Doctrines. The Alliance is orthodox trinitarian in belief. Its officers call it "strictly" evangelical. It has no official creed, its members worshiping Christ as Saviour, Sanctifier, Healer, and Coming Lord. They accept as missionaries persons from other denominations provided that they be in accord with the specific standards required by the Alliances for missionary work. The Alliance also receives contributions from members of other churches who are in sympathy with its aims.

Worship and Organization. Worship is informal, determined locally. The government of the Alliance is congregational, with each local unit described as "self-directing." A general council of representatives of the local congregations meets annually to transact such minimum business as is of common interest.

CHRISTIAN CHURCHES (DISCIPLES OF CHRIST) AND CHURCHES OF CHRIST

These two large, distinctly American religious bodies have a common origin in several local movements that culminated in the formation of a Christian Association at Washington, Pennsylvania, in 1809. The "First Church of the Christian Association of Washington" was organized in 1810 under the leadership of Thomas Campbell and his son, Alexander. Their followers were popularly termed "Campbellites."

Thomas Campbell had been a minister of the Secession Branch of the Presbyterian Church in Ireland. In Pennsylvania the Campbells at first endeavored to work together with local Presbyterian and Baptist churches, but without success. Their plea was for a return to the Bible alone, without any "human innovations," such as creeds or other symbols or formulas. They also proclaimed the essential unity of the Church of Christ, asserting that there was no place for uncharitable divisions or schisms and that they did not wish to found a new denomination. Their statements received little public attention at first, although Barton W. Stone, another "Seceder" Presbyterian minister, joined the Campbells in 1832.

Their teachings spread throughout the Middle West. The issues of the Civil War somewhat disunited the local congregations that had developed, but no major division occurred. Then, as the movement grew, it split into parties advocating special emphases. One group, for example, opposed the use of instrumental music in church (locally called the "anti-organ faction"); another opposed contributions to the organization of foreign missions or of local church associations for missionary work. By the beginning of the twentieth century there were only two main groups: one, the more conservative, was known as the Churches of Christ, the other as the Disciples of Christ. In some communities the fact that both of these bodies are often called Christian Churches perplexes those not members of these churches.

Doctrines. Neither of these religious bodies has an official creed. Baptism is by immersion, and the Lord's Supper is celebrated every Sunday morning. Although they have no written creed, both bodies appear to subscribe to the divine inspiration of the Scriptures, the revelation of God through the threefold Father, Son, and Holy Spirit, the incarnation of Christ, and His resurrection and ascension.

Worship and Organization. Worship is informal, generally determined by the local church. Each of these religious bodies has a congregational form of government, with all authority centered in the local church, which is empowered to ordain ministers, both men and women being ordained.

The International Convention of Christian Churches (Disciples of Christ) has various boards and agencies that maintain home and foreign missions for the denomination, as well as educational, social welfare, and foreign relief programs. A convention is held annually, attended by those members of the local churches who can and wish to be present. Those attending thus have personal rather than representative status. The Convention has no authority over the local churches.

The Churches of Christ have no general organization. Some of the local churches pool their resources, raising money to send missionaries abroad. The missionaries have established churches in Mexico and other countries of Latin America, Italy, Africa, and the Far East. Some communication is maintained among the local churches and members through several periodicals.

CHRISTIAN SCIENCE

Christian Science is the religion founded on the teachings of Jesus Christ as interpreted by Mary Baker Eddy (1821–1910). Early in life she studied theology as well as the mental and emotional development of individuals. She became convinced that all causation came from God, whom she regarded as Divine Mind. In 1866, Mrs. Eddy has recounted, she recovered almost instantaneously from a serious injury after reading of a healing by Jesus in the Gospel of Matthew. This event she regarded as the beginning of Christian Science.

Mrs. Eddy began to teach at Lynn, Massachusetts, and in 1875 issued the first edition of her book, *Science and Health, With Key to the Scriptures,* which has gone through countless editions. As she taught and read, she became convinced that a church was necessary for securing co-operation among those calling themselves

Christian Scientists. Accordingly, she established the Church of Christ, Scientist, in Boston in 1879 to commemorate "the work and works of our Master" and to reinstate "primitive Christianity and its lost art of healing."

Doctrines. This church regards the teachings of the Bible as a science whose adoption and application heal the body by means of mental and spiritual powers and processes. But this science is not restricted to the healing of the body or of the sick: the principles of this religion apply to every human need. Moreover, the practice of Christian Science must not be confined to the mental or intellectual sphere; it is authentically mental only if it is truly spiritual.

Further, Christian Science is defined as "divine metaphysics," "the law of God, and the law of Good, demonstrating the divine principle and the rule of universal harmony." God is thus "All in All." He is the divine principle "of all that really is." Jesus Christ is the "Way Shower." Christ's chief work is the Atonement, the "exemplification of man's unity with God, whereby man reflects divine Truth, Life, Love." Sin, sickness, and death are considered unreal—delusions of the human mind.

Worship. Local churches are required to follow the form of worship prescribed by the Mother Church, Boston. The principal constituent of the Sunday service, morning and evening, is the lesson-sermon, prepared by a Committee of the Mother Church. It is read as formulated by two readers who stand facing the congregation and read from the lesson-sermon alternately. The first reader also repeats passages from Mrs. Eddy's book, while the second reader alternates with selections from the Bible. At testimony meetings, conducted by the first reader on Wednesday evenings, members are invited to testify publicly to ways in which they have been healed or reformed by Christian Science. The local churches also arrange for public lectures at convenient times.

The trained readers and practitioners employed by Christian Science churches are required to become members of the Mother Church after having had special training. The leaders and practitioners, whose duty it is to heal and help rank-and-file members, must acknowledge that their power comes from the Divine Mind. They must accept the scriptural dictum: "I can of my own self do nothing" (John 5:30). Both men and women are eligible for appointment as practitioners.

Organization. The local churches have the right of self-government, but, as stated above, they must offer the prescribed form and content of worship. The Mother Church is controlled by a Board of Directors, the governing body of the denomination. Membership in the local churches is open to anyone (the minimum age is twelve) of Christian character who believes in and affirms that he understands Christian Science.

CHURCHES OF GOD

The fact that the term *Church of God* is used by many denominations can sometimes be rather confusing. One way of identifying these religious bodies of similar name is to attach the name of the headquarters city—for example, *Church of God* (*Anderson, Indiana*), one of the largest of these churches. These churches (with only one exception) are of distinctly American origin: they were born of revivals.

Doctrines. The Churches of God emphasize evangelism, missions, and stewardship. Major activities include frequent revival meetings and educational programs in Sunday schools.

Characteristics of Some Churches of God. The only church with a European connection was a *Seventh Day Church of God,* observing the Sabbath on Saturday, which was established at Newport, Rhode Island, in 1671 by Stephen Mumford, a recent arrival from England. The fact that this church was connected with the Mill Yard Church of God, an old congregation of London, is shown by correspondence between the two in 1680. This body was reorganized at Salem, West Virginia in 1933.

Another *Church of God* (*Cleveland, Tennessee*) was formed in 1886 by persons convinced that existing denominations were not in strict accord with Scripture and that new beginnings were necessary. The first new congregation adopted the name *Christian Union;* in 1902 this was changed to the *Holiness Church;* and in 1907 the name *Church of God* was adopted. Since then the denomination has grown steadily so that it now has members in almost all states of the Union. It is in general accord with the teachings of the Methodists. There is no official creed, the emphasis being on the individual—his regeneration and sanctification—and on "speaking in tongues" (see Glossary). The church member must "be born again." Worship is informal, while church government is a combination of congregational and episcopal forms.

The *Church of God* (*Anderson, Indiana*) regards itself perhaps as more of a movement within the church at large than as a denomination. It strives for restoration of the New Testament standards of life and faith and for Christian unity. This church was founded about 1880 under the leadership of D. S. Warner, a follower of John Winebrenner, who was originally an adherent of the German Reformed Church, but left that body to found the Churches of God. Warner and his followers felt that the churches they knew were restricted too much by human organizations and ecclesiasticism. They were strongly evangelistic and proposed to place their organization more directly under God's rule. In doctrine, this body is orthodox trinitarian. Its form of government is congregational, and worship is informal as decided locally. Ministers are ordained by those already in service.

The *Assemblies of God,* another comparatively large body, originated in extensive revivals during 1906 and 1907. The local groups developed an interest in strictly evangelistic missions at home and abroad. Contact between the local units was soon regarded as essential. About a hundred persons, mostly ministers, met at Hot Springs, Arkansas, in 1914 and resolved to establish a body devoted to "Bible order, system, and evangelism." The doctrine is orthodox trinitarian, with special emphasis on divine healing, "speaking in tongues," and the imminent second coming of Christ. Church government is a combination of congregational and presbyterian systems (see Presbyterians). Worship is nonliturgical.

CONGREGATIONALISTS

American congregationalism was an outgrowth of Separatist movements in England. Toward the end of the sixteenth century a school of thought developed there in opposition to the state church, holding that the establishment could not be reformed and that the only course for the dissenter was to separate himself from it.

Separation became Congregationalism in 1604 with the formation of a small, new group at Scrooby, England. The pastor, John

Robinson, was forced to flee the country with his congregation, emigrating to Holland in 1608, where he issued pamphlets attacking the English ecclesiastical system. After twelve years in Leiden, Robinson encouraged a number of Separatists, the Pilgrims, to emigrate to America, where the first Congregational Church was established in Plymouth, Massachusetts, in 1620. The church of the Puritans of Massachusetts Bay and that of the Pilgrims of Plymouth were subsequently confederated, thus establishing American Congregationalism. An association of local Congregational churches came into being as early as 1648.

Congregationalism spread westward rapidly. Each local church determined its own form of worship and organization, which were centered in a general council meeting for fellowship and transaction of common business. Congregationalists have always been prominent in the fields of home missions and education (especially in behalf of the Negroes after the Civil War). A number of mergers have helped to enlarge the membership. The Evangelical Protestant Church of North America merged with Congregationalism in 1924; and the General Convention of the Christian Church joined in 1931, when the name Congregational Christian Churches was adopted. In 1961 the Congregational Christian Churches merged with the Evangelical and Reformed Church to form the United Church of Christ (which see), but some local Congregational Churches which refused to join this merger formed a National Association of Congregational Churches and a Conservative Conference of Congregational Churches. American Unitarianism (see Unitarians and Universalists) was born out of Congregationalism.

EASTERN CHURCHES

The Holy Eastern Orthodox Church is a descendant of the church of the Byzantine Empire. It was founded in Alaska through the missionary zeal of a Russian trader named Glotov and was active prior to the purchase of that territory (then known as Russian America) by the United States in 1867. It is reported that in 1759 Glotov baptized several adherents and that in 1774 a certain Schelehoff (or Scheleoff) baptized forty others. In 1792 the Holy Synod of Russia sent to Alaska a mission of eight monks who baptized some twelve thousand persons within ten years. Other missionaries immigrated from Russia, including one who later became Bishop Innocent. The Bishop established a center at Sitka in 1824; in fact, the Cathedral that is still standing in Sitka was built under his direction. The eccelesiastical See was transferred in 1872 to San Francisco, where the membership included many Russians, Serbians, and Greeks.

A number of Eastern Churches were established in the United States as the result of immigration from nations of the Middle East to cities along the eastern seaboard. The Greeks, for example, began to arrive in considerable numbers in the 1890's. They felt the need of religious services and petitioned the Holy Synod of Greece and the Ecumenical Patriarchate of Constantinople for assistance. From time to time, priests were sent from the Middle East to found parishes in the larger cities and to visit groups in the smaller centers as frequently as possible. Nevertheless, there was no central organization in America (each priest being responsible to the church authorities abroad) until 1922, when the Greek Archdiocese of North and South America was finally established in New York City. The Greek Archdiocese is now the largest Eastern Orthodox body in the United States. In much the same way as the Greeks, immigrants from many other nations secured priests and organized Eastern Churches in the United States.

These autonomous churches regard themselves as the direct heirs and conservators of the churches of the Middle East in the Apostolic era. Some of the bodies use the term "Catholic" in their official names, while others, which merely imply that they are "Catholic" without explicit identification as such, are sometimes referred to collectively as "the Old Church." The patriarchs of Constantinople (Istanbul), Alexandria, Antioch, and Jerusalem are leaders of the earliest established churches, the first mentioned serving as the Ecumenical Patriarch.

Doctrines. The Eastern Churches recognize Christ as the head of the Church. The sources of their doctrines are the Holy Scripture, traditional beliefs and practices, and the decrees of the first seven Ecumenical Councils. (The first of these councils took place in Nicea in A.D. 325, the seventh, or second Nicene, council in A.D. 787). The Orthodox churches do not recognize the primacy of the Bishop of Rome as Pope. They recite an early version of the Nicene Creed which states the belief that the Holy Ghost proceeds from the Father alone (the words, "and from the Son" were added later by the Western Church). The Orthodox churches honor Mary as the Mother of God and affirm the doctrine of the Virgin Birth of Christ but deny the Roman Catholic doctrine of the Immaculate Conception. They insist upon the necessity for good works as well as faith.

Worship. The form of worship is liturgical. The liturgy is usually sung in the church, the congregation standing (or occasionally moving about) during the long service. The sacraments are the same as those of the Roman Catholics. Confession is less common than in the Roman Catholic Church. Candidates for the priesthood may marry before ordination but not afterwards. There are monastic orders, from whose members the bishops are usually chosen. Religious education of children is carried on by the parishes.

Organization. The Eastern Churches have an episcopal form of government, with synods that are convened at regular intervals. Ordination of priests is a function of the bishop. The priest is in charge of the local parish under the supervision of the bishop, organizing much of the social life of the parish and directing religious education as well as worship.

EPISCOPAL CHURCHES

(See PROTESTANT EPISCOPAL CHURCH; METHODISTS.)

ETHICAL CULTURE

The Ethical Culture Movement was initiated by Felix Adler, who founded the New York Society for Ethical Culture in 1876. Adler, son of a rabbi, was a teacher of religion and a distinguished philosopher.

Doctrines. Ethical Culture has no formal doctrine. The founder and other leaders have said that they revere the best in the traditional faiths and endeavor to interpret ethical teachings in such a way as to develop man's spiritual life and purpose today. Thus the movement draws on religious heritage as well as the wisdom of the philosophers. One purpose of the movement is to enable man to become aware of the worth of human personality, the uniqueness of every human being, the interdependence of human lives, and the possibilities inherent in their creative relationships.

Worship and Organization. At the Sunday morning meetings there are readings, lectures, and music; the details are determined locally by each society and its leader. Local societies are altogether autonomous, electing their own leaders. They administer elementary and secondary schools open to all pupils, irrespective of their religious affiliations. Societies have been organized in the United States, Europe, and Japan. The national organization in the United States is the American Ethical Union.

EVANGELISTIC ASSOCIATIONS

These associations of local churches are generally characterized by their zeal in conducting evangelistic and missionary programs. It is their emphasis (rather than their doctrines, which are broadly evangelical and Protestant) that distinguishes them.

Samuel H. Froehlich founded the Apostolic Christian Church (Nazarean) in Switzerland in the 1830's; shortly thereafter, his followers came to the United States and established churches in Ohio and Illinois. Later, in 1897, Benedict Weymouth, a Swiss minister, founded congregations among German Swiss immigrants; these are now organized as the Apostolic Christian Church of America, most of whose members are in the Middle West. The Apostolic Faith Mission began as the outcome of revivals in the Middle West in 1900. The other bodies in this group also originated in the Middle West in the late nineteenth and early twentieth centuries.

All the bodies in this group are comparatively small. In addition to those mentioned above, the Christian Congregation, the Church of God (Apostolic), the Metropolitan Church Association, the Missionary Church Association, and the Pillar of Fire are among the most widely known.

FEDERATED CHURCHES

In federated churches, which are local institutions found more often in rural than in urban communities, two or more Protestant congregations unite for central administration of their activities. Each of the combining units retains its connection with its own denominational body and has such separate meetings as are required to maintain the connection. The congregations in a federation meet regularly for worship, religious education, and social activities. They agree in advance on the form or forms of worship, the method of choosing a minister, and the curriculum for religious education. A single officer representing the federation handles the receipts and disbursements of the member churches, except that each denominational unit is expected to take care of its own charitable funds, sending them to the proper denominational official.

The first federated church appears to have been established in Massachusetts in 1897. Many others were subsequently organized in the other New England states. It is probable that at least one-third of all federated churches are located in New England.

Sometimes economic pressure was the determining factor, small churches not having the resources to maintain a pastor of their own. Another factor has been the opinion of laymen, favoring co-operation and unity among denominations. Some denominational officials have also encouraged federation.

Most of the federations comprise only two co-operating denominations, those having more than three being rare indeed. Probably three-fourths of the existing federations have been sanctioned by four denominations: Congregational Christian Churches (now United Church of Christ); Baptists; Methodists; and Presbyterians.

FRIENDS (QUAKERS)

Several members of the Society of Friends in England migrated to Massachusetts in 1656 but were denied admission—in fact, no Friends were admitted to the colony until 1724. Similar "trying experiences" attended efforts of the British group to gain admission to Virginia and Connecticut. Rhode Island received them more cordially, and they also obtained permission from the authorities to settle in New York, New Jersey, and Maryland. The principal Quaker settlement in America was established in Philadelphia under the leadership of William Penn, who had come there from England in 1682 for this purpose.

The Friends, who now are a group or family of religious bodies, trace their beginnings to the witness of George Fox (b. 1624), a native of Fenny Drayton, Leicestershire. Fox, who even as a young student had reflected long and hard concerning spiritual problems, rejected the emphasis upon mere religious forms, insisting that the divine power within the individual would enable him to live according to the will of God, to have direct communication with God, and to make outward life consistent with inner profession. This was then a highly unpopular doctrine among members of the religious institutions of England.

Fox organized a little group known for a time as "Children of Truth," "Children of Light," and "Friends of Truth," until they finally adopted the name, "Religious Society of Friends," to which the phrase "commonly called Quakers" was sometimes appended. The appellation Quakers is said to have originated with a British judge who so referred to them when George Fox called on him to "tremble [quake] at the word of the Lord."

The Friends around Fox traveled far and wide, teaching and preaching—in Britain, Europe, the West Indies, and North America. Like many other innovators, at first they seemed not to have wanted to form "another organization." But one developed, perhaps before they were aware of it.

Doctrines. The Friends have no formal creed, but emphasize the Light within. They worship in simple meeting-houses. They are committed to work for peace and to the doctrine of nonresistance in the face of violence. For this reason, many of the Friends refuse to participate in any form of military service or in direct support of war activities.

Worship. Two types of worship are followed. In one type, the meeting is "unprogrammed," with only a time and place being set for worship; the members remain silent until one of them decides to speak. In the other type, the meeting is presided over by ministers employed to conduct worship on an informal basis and to direct certain other functions accepted by the group as proper activities for bodies associated with the Protestant ministry.

Organization. The Friends have a fully democratic form of organization. As a rule, the local group transacts business at "Monthly Meetings," but it frequently postpones decisions on moot questions for long periods until a large measure of agreement has been reached. "Quarterly Meetings" are held with other groups in the same district and "Yearly Meetings" with those in the same region.

Welfare Activities. It is the policy of the Friends to work together and with other religious bodies to initiate and carry on extensive programs of relief and rehabilitation both at home and abroad. The American Friends Service Committee was organized in 1917 and has since been one of the world's most active agencies in work of this nature.

FUNDAMENTALISTS

Several of the central Protestant organizations adhere to doctrines and points of view generally known as "Fundamentalists," as do numerous local Protestant churches and many individual ministers. Perhaps the earliest Fundamentalists organization in the United States was one established about 1910 which, though no longer in existence, set a precedent that has continued to guide later bodies of this kind in various denominations.

Doctrines. The Fundamentalists reject the idea of any critical study or reinterpretation of the Scriptures, stress the literal interpretation of the Bible, and hold steadfast to faith in the Virgin Birth of Christ, in His physical resurrection, in His eventual physical return to earth, and in His substitutionary atonement.

Organization. During the past half-century, several Protestant denominations have been involved in bitter controversies between Fundamentalist members and opposing "modernist" groups. Recently, in some of the larger denominations, these violent storms have abated somewhat as many local Fundamentalist churches (e.g., some in the American Baptist Convention) withdrew from the central bodies to form or to join smaller denominations. One of the new associations, the Independent Fundamental Churches of America was organized in 1930. Among the interdenominational agencies with a Fundamentalist emphasis are the National Association of Evangelicals, the American Council of Christian Churches, and the International Council of Christian Churches.

HOLINESS BODIES

Several relatively small religious bodies professing the original Wesleyan doctrine (which emphasizes the individual's aspirations for a holy life together with evangelistic zeal) use the term "Holiness" as part of their official, or legal, names.

Holiness bodies among the Methodists include the Holiness Methodist Church, established in Grand Forks, North Dakota, in 1909; the Holiness Church of God, founded in Madison, North Carolina, in 1920; the Fire Baptized Holiness Church organized in Atlanta in 1889; and the Fire-Baptized Holiness Church (Wesleyan), which came into being about 1890 as a result of the intensive preaching of holiness doctrine among the Methodists of southeastern Kansas. (See Methodists.)

Pentecostal Holiness bodies include the Emanuel Holiness Church, organized in Whiteville, North Carolina, in 1953; the Pentecostal Fire-Baptized Holiness Church, formed by local churches in Georgia in 1918; and the Pentecostal Holiness Church, which grew out of revivals in the South and the Middle West from 1895 to 1900. (See Pentecostal Assemblies.)

The Holiness body known as the Churches of God, Holiness, originated in Georgia in 1914. (See Churches of God.)

INDEPENDENT CHURCHES

Independent local churches are those not formally affiliated with any other religious body. Prior to the First World War, there were forty of these independent groups (usually called Union Churches) in Massachusetts alone. After the war, vigorous movements developed to organize so-called "community churches" not connected with any denomination. Some local denominational churches, in order to achieve the status of complete union, severed relations with their denominations. (There seems to be no recent enumeration of the independent churches; but see the Summary of Statistics for data taken from the Census of Religious Bodies.)

These community churches should not be confused with federated churches (which see, above) or with certain denominational churches that use the term "community" in their names. The independent church groups may be formed primarily to carry on nonsectarian endeavors or to consolidate local church work, thus eliminating weaker units, such as those unable to pay the salary of a minister or to administer a desired program satisfactorily. Another motivating purpose may be the desire to meet social needs of the community more effectively than might be possible if activities were to be guided by traditional creeds or by policies of a conventional religious organization.

Forms of worship and types of organization vary considerably among the independent churches, inasmuch as each group decides upon these matters for itself.

INDIAN RELIGIOUS INSTITUTIONS

Forms of religion among American Indians have ranged from the most primitive to well-organized priestly systems. But they have all had one element in common: religion has permeated the everyday life of the Indian. He has been constantly aware of the unknown, the mysterious, the threatening, in the universe around him, regarding these as supernatural, and his religion has consisted largely of his responses to the supernatural. The American Indian's apprehension of things spiritual was usually divorced from practical ethics. The tribe or family dealt with the ordinary problems of human relations independently of religious prescriptions and ceremonials. Only in the more advanced cultures did the priest deal with human conduct, and then merely to threaten offenders with supernatural punishment. It was a generally accepted belief that the spirits would inflict punishment upon any family which failed to observe the rules for the performance of religious ceremonies.

For many years the religions of American Indians have been subject to a process of change until today the following three choices confront them: to retain the traditional emphases in religion; to follow some middle course of adaptation; or to adopt Christianity, the religion of the white man.

Traditional Beliefs. The traditional elements of Indian religious doctrine have centered in the following: mana; taboo; belief in spirits; visions; and totemism.

Mana was the name for an invisible force pervading the universe, with power to influence places, objects, and human beings.

Taboo, a corollary of mana, has been just as widely accepted. The taboo system wards off impending dangers from negative mana. To achieve this purpose the individual may withdraw from bodily activity or from social intercourse—for example, by going into seclusion, by fasting, or by abstaining from speech, from touching his head, or from allowing water to touch his lips.

Belief in spirits has become common to all American Indian religions. Spirits of the dead were regarded as existing in a shadowy afterworld, to which both the good and the bad were consigned. The living might supply them with food for the journey. The houses belonging to the departed might be destroyed to prevent the spirits of the dead from returning to live in them. Also common among Indian peoples has been the notion that spirits exist in plants, animals, and the forces of Nature.

Visions were sought as a means of assuring the individual that the supernatural powers would grant him the good fortune he needed. The individual might undergo torture in order to induce visions, or he might go into seclusion for the same purpose, or, in some tribes, he might pray and fast in his search of a vision that would bring supernatural aid.

The shaman, or medicine man, was the member of the tribe who possessed special powers of communication with the supernatural, chiefly for curing illness. The shaman has been termed the "archvisionary." Positive therapeutic results were often obtained if the patient had great faith in the shaman and his methods.

When their religious ceremonies had become well organized, the Indian tribes made use of a priestly official who took care of sacred objects and conducted rituals deemed necessary for procuring abundant crops, good weather, assistance in war, and safety in travel.

Totemism was highly developed among the Indians of the Pacific Northwest. (The word is of American Indian origin.) According to this belief, which is shared by many other primitive peoples, a tribe or an individual is thought to have a unique relationship with a plant, an animal, or an inanimate object—his totem. The totem and the man may be thought to have a common ancestor. There may be a prohibition against killing or eating one's totem. Those who have the same totem, "totem kin," are forbidden to intermarry. In the Northwest, the Indians erect buildings and set up poles decorated elaborately with figures of a totem, just as some white families have used a coat of arms.

A Middle Course. Indians who reject many traditional doctrines may choose a middle course which combines the ancient Indian customs with Christian ethical teachings but without accepting Christian theology. One religion along these lines was started by Handsome Lake, an Iroquois; another was established (on Puget Sound) by John Slocum, who blended traditional Indian with Christian concepts into what was generally regarded as a Shaker religion.

The most widely accepted of the middle-course religions is the Peyote, organized in 1918 as the Native American Church. Combining traditional Indian practices with certain modern ethical ideals, it carries on organized activities in twelve states. At its meetings beads of peyote, a mescal cactus, are passed around, and each worshiper is expected to eat eight beads, which are said to produce minor physical changes and "color visions." Activities at meetings include songs, prayers, and ceremonials.

Christian Church Members. It is estimated that about half of the more than 500,000 American Indians are members of Christian churches, equally divided between Protestants and Roman Catholics. For centuries churches have maintained numerous missions and schools to serve the American Indian. The Roman Catholics have made many converts among the Pueblo Indians, the Presbyterians among the Pimas.

INFORMAL FELLOWSHIPS

Among leading informal fellowships, the following merit special attention here: Alcoholics Anonymous; the Oxford Group (or Moral Re-Armament group); the Full Gospel Business Men's Fellowship International; and groups known as Naturalistic Humanists.

Alcoholics Anonymous. A prominent clergyman has referred to this organization as the only one he knows in which agnostics, Jews, Catholics, and Protestants get along harmoniously "on a religious basis." Established in 1935 by a former alcoholic, it is an organization devoted to the cause of mutual aid. It emphasizes religious teachings, such as "I am my brother's keeper" and "there is a Power greater than ourselves," basic doctrines deemed helpful to victims of alcoholism. Motivated by these teachings, the founder, assisted by a physician who had been an alcoholic (they had helped each other to remain sober for four years) set about forming the organization and soon had a first group of a hundred followers.

It is reported that there are now more than seven thousand groups in seventy nations.

Alcoholics Anonymous units are to be found in scores of American cities and towns from coast to coast. Regular evening monthly meetings are held, at which the Lord's Prayer is recited. The alcoholic who applies for admission is not asked to take a pledge, but he is urged to take twelve steps, in which surrender to God and a desire for spiritual awakening are continually stressed. Members are expected to answer calls for help and in fact to provide personal care for any fellow alcoholic attempting to abstain. Anonymity is considered the spiritual foundation of the movement because it places principles above personalities.

Oxford Group (or Moral Re-Armament Group). This fellowship was established by Frank Buchman (1878–1961), a Lutheran clergyman who stressed personal evangelism through small group meetings, often called "house parties." Working at first with students of colleges in the eastern United States, Buchman then went to England, where he held meetings of small groups of university students, including some at Oxford. The name "Oxford Group" was attached to the movement and was retained by the founder. (This name did not occasion great pleasure at Oxford University, inasmuch as the movement had no connection with it; and it should also not be confused with the Oxford Movement of the early nineteenth century that led to formation of the High Church party in the Anglican communion.)

Moral Re-Armament is the name now used in the United States. The emphasis is still on change within the person: new men will create new nations and a new world. Public confession of sin is one of the measures utilized in seeking God's guidance to meet the issues of life; another is a period of silence observed at local group meetings. The teaching stresses absolute honesty, purity, unselfishness, and love as the way to truly Christian living. Both in Europe and in the United States, large meetings of the membership have been attended by noted personalities from the principal nations of the world.

Full Gospel Business Men's Fellowship International. This organization is generally regarded as a fellowship rather than as a church. It began in the early 1950's as an association of persons in the Pentecostal bodies, but more recently many new adherents have come from other denominations. It professes to provide a bridge between the Pentecostals and adherents of other religious traditions.

The Fellowship holds revival meetings and personal evangelistic consultations. When conversions are made, the converts are asked either to join churches of their choice or to return to those with which they have been affiliated. A purpose of the evangelistic efforts is to achieve the "infilling of the Holy Spirit" in the person.

One of the basic doctrines of the Fellowship, like that of the Pentecostal bodies, is the belief that "speaking in tongues" or "speaking in other languages" is evidence of the "infilling of the Holy Spirit." Members assert that the term *tongues* refers to all the thousands of languages spoken by the peoples of the earth.

In addition to "speaking in tongues," the "infilling of the Holy Spirit" is also said to induce other gifts, such as interpretation of the tongues, prophecy, working of miracles, awareness of spirits, casting out of devils, and powers of healing.

The modern revival movement is said to have started during the late 1890's and early 1900's at various places, chiefly in the Middle West (see Pentecostal Assemblies). The revival movement led to the organization of several denominations, which subsequently entered into informal association with one another.

Naturalistic Humanists. Naturalistic humanism is a faith probably subscribed to by a large proportion of the "intellectuals" of this and other countries. Most of its adherents do not belong to any religious organization. In fact, naturalistic humanism has been called a nonecclesiastical religion that is very different from organized religion as the latter is generally understood.

The term *humanism* has been variously defined. Sometimes it has been used to designate an emphasis or point of view accepted by certain members in established denominations. It has been associated with Ethical Culture and with Unitarianism.

Severe critics of naturalistic humanism in its current manifestations consider it to be an atheistic doctrine, while other critics call it an agnostic one. But its adherents claim that naturalistic humanism cannot be stated so simply. Although committed neither to a formal creed nor to fixed procedures at meetings, many present-day humanists would probably agree on the following assertions: that one should reject the main ideas of theism, deism, modernism, and New Thought; that man must try to understand and live with the laws of Nature; and that, as some have put it, Nature is "eternally self-existent, uncreated, and the ground of all life."

Adherents of this movement hold that man is the highest form of life, has an obligation to work for human welfare, and will make progress and solve problems that may now seem insoluble. They advocate various co-operative efforts to achieve a just social order.

Many humanists believe that their faith will spread as mankind establishes unprejudiced education. Leading philosophers, literary figures, and social workers are to be found in the ranks of the humanists.

The American Humanist Association, a "nonsupernatural organization" with local chapters, issues its own publications.

INTERNATIONAL CHURCH OF THE FOURSQUARE GOSPEL

This denomination was established in Los Angeles in 1927 by the Canadian evangelist Aimee Semple MacPherson. Prior to the First World War, she had served as a missionary in Hong Kong, and after the war she conducted numerous evangelistic meetings in that city.

Returning to the United States in 1917, she had become the victim of a serious illness from which, she reported, she was miraculously delivered. It was at this time that she said she received a command from God to go forth to preach the gospel, and she held many revival meetings throughout the United States. She considered herself one of the leaders in the "full gospel" movements which were then gaining numerous adherents. While on one of her extended tours, she became convinced that God was summoning her to California. Consequently, she settled in Los Angeles, preaching the "foursquare gospel" to multitudes of enthusiastic listeners. Financial support from her followers enabled her in 1923 to arrange for the construction in that city of the Angelus Temple, a center of worship which became the headquarters of the denomination that she founded four years afterward. Today there are churches in all parts of the United States.

Doctrines. The beliefs of this body are broadly Protestant and trinitarian, with special emphasis on divine healing, as originally set forth by the evangelist founder. The members accept the sacraments of baptism and the Lord's Supper. Belief in the second coming of Christ to earth is regarded as one of the obligations of church membership.

Worship and Organization. The denomination does not prescribe the order of worship, which is informal and is locally determined.

The governing body of the denomination is a General Assembly, at which the ordained ministers are the voting members. A board of directors administers affairs between meetings of the assembly. The directors plus other designated ministers constitute an Ordination Board which examines the qualifications of applicants for the ministry and evangelism. There is also a Missionary Board which promotes home missions and foreign missions. Each of the local churches is governed by a council consisting of the pastor and four or six members elected by the congregation at an annual meeting.

JEHOVAH'S WITNESSES

The native American religious movement, Jehovah's Witnesses, was founded by Charles Taze Russell, a layman, in 1872 in Pittsburgh. Russell had been both a Presbyterian and a Congregationalist, but had become uncertain in his faith. He met with a few friends to "consider the Scripture's relation to the coming of Christ and His Kingdom." Russell also learned of the Adventists and was so impressed by their belief in the second coming of Christ that this was the one religious body he did not condemn. In 1909 the headquarters of the movement was moved to Brooklyn, which has since become the center of world-wide activities.

Doctrines. Jehovah's Witnesses, now organized extensively in the United States and in more than one hundred other countries, believe that the Bible plainly teaches that an old world has ended and that the Lord Jesus Christ is making preparations to return to earth. He will then destroy the organization of Satan and establish a complete state of righteousness on earth. In this Kingdom those who will have survived Armageddon will carry out Jehovah's mandate to people the earth with a righteous race.

Thus the Kingdom, the Government of God, will be on earth. There will be no oppression, no misrule, and there will be peace on earth forever. The attitude of the Witnesses toward present governments is neutral, because they consider all existing political institutions hopeless. Witnesses separate themselves as far as possible from these institutions. They emphasize that, though neutral, they are not pacifists but fight only for God.

The Witnesses assert that they carry on the original faith of the Bible, the worship of Jehovah. They say that the Bible contains God's word of truth. They believe the Bible implicitly and endeavor to follow its commandments. In order to become a Witness, one must make an unconditional personal dedication to the will of God and then proceed faithfully to do His will.

Worship. Worship is conducted locally in numerous Kingdom Halls. In these halls the services conform to the austerity of the structure. The believers meet for worship as well as for study and other activities. The person in charge is known as the congregation servant. Witnesses observe the rites of baptism and the Lord's Supper. Everyone is welcome at the service, no offering being collected. Witnesses are opposed to the established branches of Christendom and carry on anticlerical activities.

Organization. The governing body is called the Watch Tower Bible and Tract Society; it is headed by a board of seven ministers. Local congregations are organized as affiliated branches, at which much attention is devoted to the distribution of literature. The Witnesses are essentially an association of ministers, all members being called ministers. They are trained not in theological seminaries, but in classes established by local congregations. The Witness also organize large regional and national assemblies, at which great numbers of new members are baptized by immersion.

JEWISH CONGREGATIONS

In 1654, when New Amsterdam (today's New York City) had only eight hundred inhabitants, a company of Jewish refugees from Brazil was permitted to land and settle. The Jews promptly set up forms of worship in their homes or in rented rooms. In 1655, the town granted them a plot of land for a cemetery. A year later the Congregation Shearith Israel (Remnant of Israel) was organized, becoming the first congregation of Judaism in North America. Another early congregation was the one founded at Newport,

Rhode Island, in 1658. By 1850 there were seventy-seven congregations in twenty-one of the thirty-one states, mainly in the larger cities.

The development of Judaism, evolving out of the spiritual experiences of the Israelites in ancient Palestine, is recorded in the Holy Scriptures of the Jews, the Old Testament of the Christian Bible. Religious experience came first; because of its vitality, a literature followed.

Toward the end of the first century A.D., most of the Jews were dispersed from Palestine to many countries of the Middle East and Europe, where, however, they preserved intact their congregations, communities, and faith, often as oppressed minorities in ghettos. Late in the nineteenth century and thereafter, large numbers of Jewish immigrants established their culture and their religion in the United States, until today about 40 per cent of the world's Jews live in this country.

Doctrines. Judaism has no formal or official creed, no single summary of its tenets. It is often called simply "a way of life." Nevertheless, it affirms certain distinctive, fundamental religious doctrines.

The central doctrine of Judaism is that God is one. God is not divided into personalities or powers. "Hear, O Israel: The Lord our God, the Lord is One," is the affirmation that every Jew is expected to proclaim daily. Judaism holds further that God is Creator, Preserver, Ruler, and Arbiter. He is God from the beginning. He is God of righteousness, mercy, love, holiness, the ideal of moral perfection. The world created by God is good—man is not subject to Satan. The human race is a single family. Many may become immortal by following the good life.

Moreover, only divine power can enable man to advance toward perfection. The aim of history is to establish a divine kingdom of truth and righteousness on earth. The Jewish people have been regarded as unique, not because they are better than other people or have a special share of the love of God. They are unique in that they have been given special responsibilities to witness to God's great name and His unity, and to give thanks for His goodness. And because of this heavy responsibility, they are taken to task more severely by God.

Such beliefs must be translated into concrete action. Thus, it is required that God be served. Righteousness and compassionate love must be shown to orphans, widows, the oppressed, offenders, and strangers.

According to other teachings of the Law, man is free to choose between good and evil, and he is responsible for his actions. There is constant need for study and education. Every father has the duty of instructing his children; furthermore, the community as a whole bears responsibility for instructing both the young and the old. Every man is under an obligation to establish a home, celibacy being justified only in exceptional circumstances. Love of country is taught. The Jew should pray for his government.

Ever since the time of Moses and the Ten Commandments, Judaism has been guided by a broad social vision and code, setting forth the ideals and standards for the good commonwealth. The social code declared the rights of man under the inspiration of God—e.g., as specified in the Biblical Commandment, "Six days shalt thou labor." The social code provided for compulsory holidays; for prompt payment of wages to the laborer; for the right to own property (although property rights are limited); and for donation of part of the harvest to succor the helpless. Love for God and for man must find expression in social justice.

Whenever the "Chosen People" failed to implement the high teachings of their codes, fortunately the great leaders, the prophets, divinely inspired, arose in Israel to lead the people back to the traditions and practices of their moral heritage. They emphatically asserted that the God who created the universe was also concerned with right relations among men.

Worship. There are three branches of Judaism in the United States: Orthodox, Conservative, and Reform (or Liberal). In many countries the great majority of congregations are Orthodox, adhering strictly to the old traditions. Conservative Judaism is a distinctly American development; it seeks a middle way between the old and the new. Reform, or Liberal, Judaism, which is now widely organized in this country, originated in Germany.

Each of the three branches of Judaism prescribes its own form of worship and has its own special prayerbook. The traditional rituals are generally followed, but, since Jewish congregations are autonomous and include numerous immigrants with diverse cultural backgrounds, some minor variations are not uncommon: for example, they may differ as to the extent to which English may be used in the services, and they may or may not allow certain types of instrumental music to accompany prayers.

Organization. The local units of Judaism are often considered congregational in form of government, for the national associations comprising representatives of local congregations have no control over the independent congregations. Moreover, some local congregations have no affiliation with the national association.

The ministry of Jewish congregations consists of rabbis, who have usually been trained at theological seminaries for their functions as preachers, teachers, and community leaders. They are ordained by two or more rabbis. National rabbinical associations meet regularly for social communion and advancement of other common interests.

The Synagogue Council of America represents both the congregational and the rabbinical organizations of all three branches of Judaism and promotes co-operation among them.

The congregations support and administer numerous Sabbath and weekday schools in which the principles of Judaism are taught. Often they encourage and assist social welfare agencies, although the latter generally run their own separate organizations. American congregations have always contributed substantially to the relief of distress and to the work of rehabilitation among needy Jews abroad. This has been particularly evident in connection with coreligionists in Israel, for ever since that state was established in 1948, American Jews have contributed large sums repeatedly to assist its development, although obviously not all of them consider themselves part of the political Zionist movement.

LATTER-DAY SAINTS (MORMONS)

The religious denomination popularly known as the Mormons originated with a group of six persons organized by Joseph Smith (at Fayette, Seneca County, in New York State) in 1830. Smith (born in Vermont in 1805) thus founded what was to become one of the larger and distinctly American religious movements.

At the early age of fourteen, Smith had become much concerned about the salvation of his soul and the true nature of the church of Christ. He was disturbed by the variety of denominations already on the American scene and their divergent views of the Scriptures.

On one significant occasion he had a vision "of great light," and two brightly illumined persons, who appeared before him, commanded him not to join any of the existing religious denominations. They added that God would soon restore the gospel, not then found in its fullness in any religious body. Months later, Smith had another vision, in which he was told of the second coming of Christ and his own responsibilities in that connection. An angel also told him where he would find plates from which the Book of Mormon could be translated. He said that he dug up the plates in 1827 and that eleven witnesses had seen them. The text of these plates, which were purportedly made of gold, stated that they were the sacred records of ancient inhabitants of the Americas. Smith dictated a translation of the writing on the plates to his secretaries (Martin Harris, Oliver Cowdry, and others).

After a series of other revelations, in one of which the priesthood of Aaron and of Melchizedek was conferred on the leaders of the little group, Smith and his followers founded the church in which they believed the full gospel to have been restored. Missionaries were sent out to enlist new believers. The group migrated westward, settling in various states, enduring and surviving persecution, and established themselves permanently at Salt Lake City, Utah. In 1844, en route to the Far West, Joseph Smith and his brother Hyrum were killed by a mob in the city jail at Carthage, Illinois.

After the murder of Joseph Smith, Brigham Young emerged as the strong leader, but a large dissident faction refused to follow him. The practice of polygamy had aroused violent opposition in communities of the Middle West where the Latter-Day Saints had tried to settle. In 1852 Brigham Young declared plural marriage to be a doctrine received by Joseph Smith in a revelation. (Marriage might be either for time or for eternity; the latter form is called "celestial.") After Congress had enacted various laws prohibiting plural marriage in the United States, the general conference of the Latter-Day Saints called on the members of the church not to contract marriages that were forbidden by law.

Doctrine. The Latter-Day Saints believe in the Bible, as correctly translated, and in the Book of Mormon as the word of God; in the gifts of prophecy, healing, and revelation; and in the return of Christ to rule the earth in person. They practice the rites of baptism and the Lord's Supper.

Worship. On the Sabbath day, several kinds of services are held. The first type of service is only for men and for boys over twelve years old. The purpose is to instruct those already ordained or about to be ordained. The second type of service is in Sunday school, at meetings, usually before noon, which members and others are invited to attend. At the opening of the school the sacrament of the Lord's Supper is offered, then those attending separate into groups to study the Bible, the Book of Mormon, and the doctrine and covenants of the Church. The third type of service, a sacrament service, takes place in the afternoon or evening at meetings to which members and nonmembers are invited. This service is devoted to the sacrament of the Lord's Supper and to a sermon on the teachings of Jesus Christ and His prophets.

Organization. The government of the church comprises the ward, the district, the stake, and the mission. The ward corresponds to the local church unit in other bodies. It has a meeting house and is under the care of a bishop and two counselors. A stake is a geographical unit consisting of a number of wards. A mission usually serves a group of states in the United States or a foreign country, in which appointed missionaries work for two-year periods. A general conference, composed of representatives from all parts of the church, is held twice a year, in the spring and the fall. The over-all organization of the church is in charge of the priesthood. A quorum of "twelve apostles" administers the work of the church, with one of the twelve designated as the president. Most of those ordained earn their living in other occupations.

The Latter-Day Saints raise money through a tithing system, every member being expected to pay one-tenth of his income to the church. They maintain an extensive welfare program to assist needy members, and support numerous missionaries overseas. Many young people devote two years of their lives to missionary service. The organization has become a large international church, which enters into every aspect of the life of its people.

LATTER-DAY SAINTS (REORGANIZED CHURCH OF LATTER-DAY SAINTS)

In 1860 Joseph Smith II, a son of the founder of the Latter-Day Saints, became leader of the Reorganized Church of Jesus Christ of Latter-Day Saints. This group from the beginning advocated monogamous marriage, claiming that the founder never sanctioned polygamy. It emphasizes a gospel of faith, repentance, baptism, laying on of hands to confer the Holy Ghost on a baptized person, the resurrection, and eternal judgment. It accepts the Bible and the Book of Mormon as the word of God.

Special stress is laid on stewardship, the brotherhood of man, and the building of Zion (the ideal community). Social reform must await individual regeneration. The bases of social relations are love, righteousness, and justice.

The general organization of this church is likewise in charge of the priesthood. There also are a general conference, district organizations, or stakes, and local branches, the last being the equivalent of the parish or congregation in other bodies. Worship takes place in the local branches.

LUTHERANS

Lutherans came to the New World as early colonists. Swedes landed on the shores of the Delaware between 1638 and 1648, but the churches established there lost contact with the mother country. A Lutheran congregation was formed on Manhattan Island in 1648 by immigrants from Germany, which was the chief source of Lutheran growth in the colonies. By 1750 there were perhaps 50,000 Lutherans in Pennsylvania alone. Later waves of Lutheran immigration brought Norwegians, Swedes, Danes, and Finns, who went directly to the Middle West.

Many of the first Lutheran colonists in America had no pastors. In response to urgent appeals, the University of Halle sent a prominent clergyman, Henry Melchior Muhlenberg, to Pennsylvania, where he established the first synod, the Ministerium of Pennsylvania. A General Synod followed in 1820, bringing unity to the organizations and signaling their independence from the bodies in Germany. New Lutheran denominations were formed to take care of increasing members of immigrants settling in the Western states.

Lutheranism in America is an offshoot of the institutions created in Europe as a result of the reforms of Martin Luther (1483–1546), whose followers insisted on using his name for the denomination even though he himself was opposed to their so doing. Luther, as an Augustinian monk, at first worked to bring about changes within the Roman Catholic Church. Once he was convinced that the reforms that he advocated could not be achieved, he concentrated on matters of faith, rather than organization. He was the most conservative of the Reformers with whom the term Reformation is now associated. He drew up a liturgical order of service and retained vestments and altars, but he sanctioned an emphasis on preaching that is not found in the Roman Catholic Church.

Luther became the popular leader of a movement that benefited from a series of historical developments. There had been Protestants before Luther. His success may be partially explained by the support he received from political and economic forces within Germany. His time was also marked by intellectual revolts against the traditional scholasticism of the Roman Catholic Church. The Reformation is often dated from October 31, 1517, when Luther nailed his Ninety-five Theses to the door of the castle church in Wittenberg. Luther was tried for heresy at the Diet of Worms in 1523, but he escaped to the Wartburg, the castle of his protector, Frederick the Wise.

Martin Luther made a translation of the entire Bible into German, a version still widely used. He also took some of the books out of the Bible used by Catholics and placed them in the Apocrypha. The books that remained are still regarded as the Bible of the Protestants of the world. The Apocrypha is either printed separately by Protestants or placed between the Old and New Testaments.

Doctrine. The Lutheran bodies of America declare that the books of the Old and New Testaments are inspired of God and constitute the sole and perfect rule of faith and life. They also accept the historic creeds (Apostles', Nicene, and Athanasian) as conveying the faith of Christians and as being in accord with the Scriptures. They further hold that the Augsburg Confession is in harmony with the Scriptures and that the Apology of the Augsburg Confession, Luther's two catechisms, the Schmalkald Articles, and the Formula of Concord (other sixteenth-century expressions of the new faith) are all faithful interpretations of the teachings of the Word of God and of the Augsburg Confession.

Justification by faith alone in Jesus Christ is regarded as the central doctrine of the Word of God, from which all other doctrines are developed. In preaching the Word of God, Law and Gospel are equally emphasized in order to achieve repentance and faith. The two recognized sacraments are those of baptism and of the Lord's Supper, which are regarded as means of grace and not mere memorials or symbols. In the bread and wine of the Lord's Supper, Lutherans believe, there is the real presence of the body and blood of the Lord Jesus Christ, which are sacramentally and supernaturally received by the partaking believer.

Worship. Lutheran worship is liturgical, formal. The rituals are rather elaborate, with careful attention to details such as colors of altar cloths and of vestments, according to the season of the church year. Applicants for church membership must receive a course of instruction based on an official catechism. Congregational singing is encouraged.

Organization. The customary form of organization has become known as the Lutheran system. Accepting democratic American points of view, Lutherans abandoned the traditional less democratic forms of state churches of northern Europe and created their own independent organizations. These comprise local congregations (the primary bodies); synods (often formed on state lines); and general organizations, or conventions. The congregations possess all powers except those delegated to state synods and general organizations. The synods ordain ministers, who preach the Gospel and administer the sacraments. In these functions all ministers have equal authority.

The congregation elects the minister, who usually holds indefinite tenure; it may dismiss him from his pastorate but it has no power to depose him from the ministry.

MENNONITES

In 1693 Mennonite pioneers in America, consisting of thirteen families from Krefeld, Germany, settled in Germantown (now part of Philadelphia), to which they had been invited by William Penn (see Friends), as refugees from religious persecution. Today there is a sizable group of Mennonite denominations in the United States.

The Mennonites take their name from Menno Simons, a Dutch Roman Catholic priest converted to Protestantism. The first Mennonite congregation was formed in Zurich in 1525 by a group who referred to themselves as Swiss Brethren but were popularly known as *Täufer* (Baptizers). They did not approve of infant baptism, and because they practiced rebaptism, they were also called *Anabaptists.* Menno Simons was rebaptized in the Netherlands in 1536, and it was then that his name became associated with this large body of Christians which eventually spread throughout the world. Opposition to the congregation persisted until in 1577 William of Orange demanded that there be no further persecution of the dissenters.

From Germantown the struggling Mennonites of 1693 and many others who followed them from Holland, Germany, and Switzerland spread out northward and westward. It may be noted that their principle of nonresistance provided better protection from Indians than did the rifles and stockades of other settlers.

Doctrines. Mennonite doctrines were formulated in a conference at Dort, Holland, in 1632. Among the eighteen Articles of the Declaration of Dort are the following: God is the creator of all things. Man fell through his disobedience. Christ, the Son of God, purchased the redemption of man through his death. The law of Christ is contained in the Gospels. Only by obedience to Christ's law is humanity saved. Repentance and conversion are necessary to salvation. Christ forbids his followers to use physical force in resisting evil or to seek revenge for unjust treatment. The use of oaths is forbidden. At the Last Judgment, the good shall be separated from the evil, the good to enter heavenly joy, the evil to depart from God's presence.

Worship. Worship is informal, as determined by the local minister and congregation. The Lord's Supper is observed twice a year. In some denominations, baptism is by immersing, in others by pouring.

Organization. In all but a few of the Mennonite bodies, the form of government is such that the local congregation is independent, with power to decide all matters. Ministers are often self-supporting, having occupations in addition to the ministry.

AMISH MENNONITES

The Conservative or Old Order Mennonites, the Amish, take their name from Jacob Amen (or Amman), a young religious leader in Alsace. In the early period of the Mennonite group he advocated the strictest adherence to the Declaration of Dort (see above). The Amish, most of them farmers, do not erect separate buildings for worship, but meet for this purpose in rooms of the members' spacious farmhouses.

The Amish prescribe a distinctive mode of dress for their members at all age levels—a style that tends to set them apart from their neighbors. As farmers they are famed for skillful cultivation without tractors or electricity, making extensive use of windmills and water power. Refusing to drive automobiles, they still travel by horse and buggy. They will not install telephones in their homes, although they do make use of public telephones to facilitate business or to protect the neighborhood.

The Amish exercise rigid discipline over members. They allow children to attend public schools only through the elementary grades. To a limited extent they co-operate with other Mennonite bodies, but ordinarily carry on their work independently of other denominations.

METHODISTS

Methodism originated in 1729 at Oxford University, where John Wesley, his brother Charles, George Whitfield, and others met regularly for religious exercises, including Bible study. They became convinced that they "could not live without holiness" and thus "they followed after it, and incited others to do so." The earnest little company was derided by fellow students as "The Holy Club," "Bible Bigots," and "Methodists." The last name, though intended as an epithet, became the preferred designation, even by those derided. The group became known as the Methodist Movement.

During these early years, Wesley came into contact with the Moravians, who were destined to influence him greatly. He met with them abroad ship in 1735 en route to America and he later visited their first American church. From the devoted Moravians Wesley received what he called a new understanding of saving faith.

Wesley recorded in his *Journal* that he went "very unwillingly on May 24, 1738, to a Society in Aldersgate Streat [London], where one was reading Luther's 'Preface to the Epistle of the Romans.' " While he was describing the change that God works in the heart through faith in Christ, he reported that "I felt my heart strangely warmed. I felt I did trust in Christ, in Christ alone for salvation; and an assurance was given me that he had taken away my sins, even mine, and saved me from the law of sin and death." After that John Wesley was "a different man."

In 1739 he met with about ten other persons in London, and out of this meeting came the "United Society."

John and Charles Wesley and George Whitfield, although ordained as clergymen of the Church of England, were regarded as preachers of new doctrines and were soon excluded from many pulpits of the Established Church. And yet both Wesleys lived and died as clergymen in good standing with the Church of England.

At the now celebrated parish of Epworth—famous because of the Wesleys—where the father of John and Charles had been the rector, John Wesley was once locked out. Thereupon he went to the churchyard, stood on his father's tombstone, and spoke to the people gathered there on the text: "The Kingdom of God is not meat and drink; but righteousness, and peace, and joy in the Holy Ghost" (Romans 14:17 in the King James Version).

"Very well, I will have all the world for my parish," was John Wesley's answer to those who would exclude him from the parishes. When they closed a thousand parishes to him, he found a thousand reasons why he should preach to the people he met in the world. His future ministry would be outside the walls of churches. John, his brother Charles, and George Whitfield preached in fields, homes, halls, and barns. Thus the Wesleys began a great evangelical revival throughout England in the eighteenth century.

As converts and adherents were received, they were organized into small societies for worship, followed by class meetings for the care and training of members. An informal circuit system was set up, with each group of several local units placed under the supervision of a lay preacher. In 1744 a conference was held at which John Wesley met his co-workers. Some of the principal features of what is now characteristic Methodist organization thus grew out of the necessities in the situation of a dissenting movement in Britain.

The first Methodist congregation in the United States was that on John Street, in New York City, founded in 1768 by Philip Embury, who had come over from Ireland with his "class meeting" of followers. John Wesley himself had spent three years (1735–

38) in Georgia as a sort of spiritual adviser to Governor Oglethorpe and missionary to the Indians. At about the same time that the John Street Church was established in New York, Robert Strawbridge, a native of Ireland, organized a small congregation in Frederick County, Maryland. In response to appeals from America, Wesley arranged for missionaries to be sent to the New World, among them Thomas Rankin and Francis Asbury.

The first annual conference of Methodists in the American colonies was held in Philadelphia in 1773. After the American Revolution Wesley wrote a letter (1784) to a gathering of his American brethren, telling them that thenceforth they would be completely separate from the British state and churches. "They are now at full liberty simply to follow the Scriptures and the primitive church."

Thereupon the Americans established the Methodist Episcopal Church, the parent body of more than a score of denominations in the United States. The Methodist Episcopal Church, South, was formed in the slaveholding states in 1845, with over 460,000 members, reflecting the divisive issue of slavery. Both the parent body and the Southern Church continued to grow. The two bodies reunited in 1939, joining with the Methodist Protestant Church to form The Methodist Church, now one of the largest religious bodies in the nation. Other well-known Methodist denominations are the Free Methodist Church of North America, the Wesleyan Methodist Church of America, and three bodies with predominantly Negro memberships: the African Methodist Episcopal Church, the African Methodist Episcopal Zion Church, and the Christian Methodist Episcopal Church.

Doctrines. The articles of religion of the parent body, the Methodist Episcopal Church, followed closely those of the Church of England. The only formal creed adopted, however, was the Apostles' Creed.

The official beliefs of the parent Methodist bodies in the United States are termed Arminian, after Jacobus Arminius, a Dutch theologian who preached more liberal doctrines of salvation than John Calvin. Arminius emphasized repetance, faith, holiness, while the stricter Calvin stressed predestination and reprobation. Methodists are trinitarian and generally believe in the fall of man, the need of repentance, freedom of the will, sanctification, future rewards and punishments, and the sufficiency of the Scriptures for rules of faith and life. The sacraments of baptism and the Lord's Supper are observed.

Worship. Some of the Methodist churches have a litany, but throughout Methodism wide liberty is generally allowed the local church and minister in arranging the order of worship.

Organization. The form of church government varies considerably among Methodist bodies. Some of the smaller denominations are altogether congregational, with no superior authority above the local church, which determines the form of worship and the details of organization. The larger bodies (the Methodist Church, the African Methodist Episcopal Church, the African Methodist Episcopal Zion Church, and the Christian Methodist Episcopal Church) all have episcopal systems, as their names indicate. The over-all organization includes the local church, the ministry, and a system of conferences comprising ministers and laymen. Bishops are elected by the conferences as administrators over churches in specific areas; they appoint the ministers within each area. The Methodist Church, the largest body of this denomination, also has district superintendents (supervised by the bishops) for administration of smaller areas. The Methodist bodies have boards for education, home and foreign missions, world relief, and other purposes.

MORMONS

(See LATTER-DAY SAINTS)

MORAVIANS

In 1457 spiritual followers of the martyrs Jan Hus (1369?–1415) and Jerome of Prague (d. 1416) formed a religious community in the deserted village of Kunewald, Moravia. This was the first of the Moravian bodies, the Brethren. The aim of this pre-Reformation church was strict obedience to scriptural teachings and to the disciplines of the Apostolic Church. Notwithstanding violent opposition, the work begun at Kunewald spread until in Luther's time there was in Bohemia and Moravia some four hundred congregations with about 150,000 adherents. During the Thirty Years' War

(1618–1648) the area was devastated and the movement was virtually destroyed, but surviving Moravians fled to Hungary, Saxony, Poland, and the Netherlands.

After a century of inactivity, the church was revivified under the sponsorship of Nicolaus Ludwig, Count of Zinzendorf, in the new village of Herrnhut, Saxony. Although Zinzendorf, a German Lutheran Pietist, wished at first only to promote a leavening movement within Lutheranism, a separate denomination emerged. Zinzendorf, meanwhile, received Lutheran ordination in Sweden.

The chief purpose of the reorganized church, the *Unitas Fratrum* (Unity of the Brethren), was to conduct evangelistic and missionary work in both the so-called "Christian" and other lands. During evangelistic work, the Brethren enrolled some converts in the larger religious bodies of Europe in the hope of developing an evangelical alliance of churches. For this reason Zinzendorf is regarded as an "ecumenical pioneer."

The Moravian settlements in America included Bethlehem, Nazareth, and Lititz, all in Pennsylvania, and Salem, now part of Winston-Salem, North Carolina. Zinzendorf visited America and aided in the founding of Bethlehem in 1741. The Moravians preached the Gospel to the Indians.

Doctrines. The Moravians have no body of doctrine peculiar to themselves. Their life and work are simply broadly evangelical, in general harmony with the central beliefs of all Protestants. They have no official creed. Their beliefs, witnesses, and teachings are found in the reports of the synods across the centuries and in the litanies that are regularly used, especially the one for Easter Sunday. The Moravian churches accept the Scriptures as containing the rules of faith and practice. They observe the sacraments of baptism and the Lord's Supper.

Organization. The form of government of the Moravian Church in America is that of a modified episcopacy or conferential body. The bishops have no dioceses, their chief function being to ordain ministers and to perform duties of a largely spiritual nature. They do not become administrators unless specially elected as such by the synod, which represents the local churches. Notwithstanding its relatively small membership the church conducts extensive foreign missions and has been consistently active in many phases of education.

In addition to the Moravian Church, which is organized into

Northern and Southern Provinces, there are Moravian congregations in Texas which still use the ancient name, Unity of the Brethren.

MUSLIMS

A few small groups of worshipers adhering to the religion of Islam are to be found in scattered communities throughout the United States. Their representatives meet from time to time in informal association. A large mosque in Washington, D.C., is probably the best-known center. It is reported to have been erected largely at the instance of Egyptian residents in the nation's capital. These followers of Islam are not to be confused with a semisecret organization known as the Black Muslims (see below), a body of American Negroes favoring segregation.

There are in New York City many Muslims who serve as members of the staffs of the missions of Arab and other nations to the United Nations; their religious activities include both private worship and occasional sessions of formal worship.

Islam is the religion founded by Muhammad (A.D. 570–632). (Note the alternative spellings, Mohammed and Mahomet.) Although their religion is popularly known as Mohammedan in the Western world, Muhammad's followers prefer the term "Muslims" and reject "Mohammedan." In their view the name of God is Allah, Muhammad being only a prophet or great teacher. Islam has no professional priesthood. Images (as aids to worship) are forbidden, but in the mosques, arabesque forms of ornament and architecture have been highly developed.

Muhammad was born in Mecca, Arabia. About his childhood and youth nothing but vague oral traditions has survived. He began his public career when he was about forty years old. He knew something of Judaism and of Christianity, as did others in Arabia at the time. These teachings influenced his later views about God's judgment and the future life. Becoming involved in a dispute over idols with officials of Mecca, he fled to Medina in 622, this date being regarded as the time of birth of the new religion. Soon thereafter Muhammad became the best-known and most powerful individual in Arabia, where he was both civil ruler and religious leader.

Muhammad rejected the Trinity of Christendom, calling instead for the worship of the one God Allah. He promised paradise for the true believer and eternal hellfire for the unbeliever. Muhammad was also deeply conscious of the primitive religion and customs of the Arabs. As the Arab world expanded after Muhammad's death, the adherents of Islam rapidly grew in numbers. Within a century after Muhammad, Islam had gained adherents in a vast area extending from India to Spain.

Doctrines. The disciples of Islam are noted for their adoration of God. Five daily prayers are expected of each believer, with the worshiper facing toward Mecca. The following are the five pillars of the religion:

(1) The daily prayer sessions for worship.

(2) Belief in the simple creed, which is stated in two forms: "There is no God but Allah, and Muhammad is the messenger (prophet) of God"; and "I believe in God, His angels, His books, and His messengers, the last day, resurrection from the dead, predestination by God, good and evil, the judgment, the balance, paradise, and hellfire."

(3) Fasting from sunrise to sunset during the lunar month of Ramadan. (This practice becomes very difficult when the lunar calendar causes Ramadan to fall in summer, with its intense heat and prolonged daylight.)

(4) Almsgiving, one of Muhammad's early teachings. (This practice includes voluntary as well as compulsory giving for relief of the poor.)

(5) Pilgrimage to Mecca, once in a lifetime, for those possessing the means to travel. (On this occasion the unity of Islam is emphasized.)

The missionary motive is also stressed, the faithful being exhorted to make converts. Today the movement is rapidly winning converts throughout Africa.

Worship. Worship in a mosque, with all the faithful turned toward Mecca, is conducted by a person appointed for the purpose. The Koran is Islam's book of Scriptures, put into its present form about twenty years after the prophet's death. Comprising numerous sections which vary widely in literary quality, it contains the utterances of Muhammad on a great multitude of subjects.

BLACK MUSLIMS

The Black Muslims of the United States are a semisecret organization of Negroes. They use the Koran, but are reported to be repudiated by orthodox Muslims. The Black Muslims are openly anti-Christian as well as anti-white. They are disciplined and militant, opposing the well-known leaders in the American Negroes' movement to abolish race prejudice and segregation.

The Black Muslims advocate resettlement of Negroes in sections of the United States that they would occupy exclusively. Their national leader, Elijah Muhammad, is said to have been born and brought up in Georgia, where his name was Elijah Poole. The group hold mass meetings in the larger cities and claim an organized following in some eighty cities. They own restaurants, food stores, and other businesses in large municipalities, such as New York City, Washington, Detroit, and Chicago.*

NAZARENES (CHURCH OF THE NAZARENE)

The Wesleyan teaching that Jesus Christ had made provision to perfect mankind in love as well as to save it from sin was the central concern of a small group who met in Providence, Rhode Island, in 1886. In 1887, after a few meetings in homes and in a rented store, they organized a Sunday school with ninety-five members and, shortly thereafter, a church with fifty-one members led by the Reverend F. A. Hillery as minister. Numerous revivals throughout the nation preceded formation of local churches.

Associations of these local churches became active under various names. In 1907 a general assembly was held in Chicago; in 1919 the present name, Church of the Nazarene, was adopted by the denomination.

Doctrines. The doctrines of the Church of the Nazarene are in accord with historical Methodism (which see). The Church emphasizes "apostolic purity" in teaching and "primitive simplicity" in

* See C. Eric Lincoln, *The Black Muslims in America* (Boston, Mass.: The Beacon Press, 1961).

worship. It holds that Jesus Christ baptizes believers with the Holy Spirit. Entire sanctification is an act of God toward the one who is truly faithful. The total experience of the sanctified individual is described in various terms, such as Christian perfection, the fullness of the blessing, and Christian holiness. The Church emphasizes divine healing of the sick. In general, the Nazarenes adhere to the central teachings of orthodox Protestant trinitarianism.

Worship. The form of worship is nonliturgical. Individuals applying for church membership are received upon their confession of faith in Christ and their promise to observe the rules that constitute the conscience of the Church. One rule, for example, prohibits use of intoxicating beverages. Baptism and the Lord's Supper are observed as ordinances.

Organization. The church government is representative, for the Nazarenes believe that this avoids the extremes of absolute congregationalist and episcopal forms. Representatives of local churches meet in a district assembly, which has authority to license and ordain ministers and elects a superintendent of the district. Delegates (elected by the districts) to the general assembly supervise denominational affairs. The assembly elects officers to represent it.

NEW JERUSALEM CHURCHES (CHURCHES OF THE NEW JERUSALEM)

The first society devoted to the teachings of Emanuel Swedenborg was formed in Baltimore in 1792. Swedenborg (born in Stockholm in 1688) became a noted and versatile scientist. After a long career as a civil servant, he was retired on a pension and devoted his remaining years to the spiritual revelation that he said had come to him. He once remarked that he had studied anatomy only in order to investigate the soul of man.

Swedenborg published his first theological treatises in 1749–56, and he continued to write on religion until his death in London in 1772. Eleven years later Robert Hindmarsh, a London printer, was attracted by Swedenborg's writings and gathered a small group around him to study them. The New Jerusalem Church was formally organized in 1787, with sixteen members, and public services were held one year later.

The religious body based on Swedenborg's teachings is sometimes known as "The New Church," but in 1817 the national organization in the United States adopted the name General Convention of the New Jerusalem. A split occurred in 1890, and a second body, The General Church of the New Jerusalem, was founded.

Doctrines. The doctrines of this church are elaborate. They teach that there is one God, the Saviour, Jesus Christ; that there is in him a nonpersonal trinity of essences: Father, Son, and Holy Spirit. The Lord Jesus Christ is the God of heaven and earth and is the only and supreme object of worship by men and angels. When an individual dies, it is held that he is raised in his spiritual body to a spiritual world. There he lives, either in heaven or in hell, depending on the character he had achieved on earth. Baptism is administered in the traditional Christian formula: "In the name of the Father, and of the Son, and of the Holy Spirit," to both children and adults. If a person is baptized in infancy, confirmation for full church membership follows in "mature years."

Worship. The form of worship is liturgical, with many chants, but local churches are free to change the order of worship. Complete books of worship are available.

Organization. The local societies possess freedom to administer local property and to elect local officers. The annual convention, which each member is authorized to attend, is an ecclesiastical, legislative, and judicial body. It maintains the orders of the ministry. A council of ministers, however, has charge of many matters related to the ministry, which includes pastors and general pastors, the latter having broad supervisory powers over the local societies.

These churches carry on missionary work both at home and abroad with use of extensive educational publications, many of them made available by the Swedenborg Foundation in New York City.

NEW THOUGHT

New Thought is a point of view (or a school of thought) rather than an organization. Its influence is found in several organizations. A principal emphasis is the belief in the "immediate availability of God," and in "conscious and practical application of spiritual thought force to the solution of human problems. . . . Every man becomes an individualized center of God Consciousness, eternally expanding."

In the United States this point of view received its impetus from Ralph Waldo Emerson's dissent from orthodoxy and from widespread opposition to Calvinism in the 1840's. The founders of New Thought had great confidence in man's intellectual powers—in the capacity of the human mind to discover truth. Among them were the Transcendalist thinkers of New England, who were greatly influenced by Oriental thought stressing the sparks of divinity in man.

Phineas P. Quimby, one of the healers consulted by Mary Baker Eddy, the founder of Christian Science (which see) is said to have contributed more than anyone else to the beginnings of the New Thought movement. Julius A. Dresser, another of Quimby's patients, became a prominent leader of the new group, and eventually Dresser's son, Horatio, became the historian of the movement.

Doctrines. In 1914 the New Thought adherents organized the International New Thought Alliance, stating one of its principal objectives as follows: "To teach the infinitude of the Supreme One, the Divinity of Man and his infinite possibilities through the creative power of constructive thinking and obedience to the voice of the Indwelling Presence which is our Source of Inspiration, Power, Health, and Prosperity."

The believers profess to teach a practical idealism. They differ sharply from Christian Science, for they do not deny the reality of the material world. The teachings of these groups on personal morality are much like those of Christian churches generally, though their emphasis is on the individual's thought rather than on his social outreach.

Worship and Organization. The Church members cite the Bible, especially the New Testament, as the main source of spiritual guidance, doctrinal teachings, and practical conduct. In local communities, New Thought may be expressed in organizations called Divine Science, or Church of Truth, or Chapel of Truth, or Institute of Religious Science. Worship and form of government are congregational.*

* See Charles S. Braden, *These Also Believe* (New York: The Macmillan Company, 1949); and *Spirits in Rebellion* (Dallas: Southern Methodist University Press, 1963).

OLD CATHOLICS

The Old Catholics are a group formed by certain communicants of the Roman Catholic Church who refused to accept the decree of the 1870 Vatican Council setting forth the dogma of papal infallibility when the Pope speaks as head of the Church on matters of faith and morals. Shortly after the Council, the dissenting bishops and theologians organized a number of Old Catholic Churches in Bavaria, Prussia, Austria, Switzerland, and the Netherlands. Small groups of American Roman Catholics expressed dissatisfaction with the Council's decrees, and some of them organized themselves as Old Catholic parishes. In Europe, however, only the Old Catholic Churches of Switzerland and of the Netherlands appear to have survived to preserve the traditions of the dissenters.

The Old Catholics in the United States are reported to have no formal connections with the European groups, despite some doctrinal similarities. They reject the idea of the supremacy and infallibility of the Pope and in their worship they make use of modified versions of Roman Catholic rituals.

PENTECOSTAL ASSEMBLIES

In Topeka, Kansas, a band of Christians, "hungry for God," called for a fast of twenty-one days to take place in December, 1899; in view of the approaching year 1900, during their fast they prayed for a great outpouring of the Holy Spirit. This they experienced with much rejoicing on December 31, 1899, when many manifestations of the working of the Holy Spirit occurred. For one, people began "speaking in tongues" (see Glossary) even as people spoke on the Day of Pentecost according to the Book of Acts. This experience was followed by revivals in Kansas and other states. One Pentecostal body today traces its origins to the fast in Topeka.

In fact, the denominations comprising the present-day Pentecostal group originated in the United States with a series of revivals in several states that started about 1895. Some of the worshipers who formed these new distinctly American denominations had been members of established religious bodies, but others had had no previous religious connections.

Doctrines. One belief common to the Pentecostals, which they regard as peculiar to themselves, is that an individual should experience a baptism of the Holy Spirit immediately after conversion. The Biblical basis for their beliefs varies. They refer to Acts 2 and the descriptions of the Day of Pentecost, as well as to Joel 2:28: "Your sons and your daughters shall prophesy, your old men shall dream dreams, your young men shall see visions." Today, the Pentecostal bodies hold that manifestation of the Holy Spirit results in "speaking in tongues." For authority they go to church history as well as to the Scriptures.

Worship and Organization. Worship is informal in the Pentecostal bodies. Their form of organization varies: some are congregational; some follow methodism, and others have a presbyterian system. For some time the various Pentecostal bodies established during the past sixty years went their own way, having little communication with other denominations, or, for that matter, with one another. Eventually, however, intergroup contacts were developed and in 1948 the Pentecostal Fellowship of North America was established, enabling representatives of the several denominations to meet and discuss their common interests.

POLISH NATIONAL CATHOLICS

A movement for independence arose among large Polish parishes of the Roman Catholic Church in the United States late in the nineteenth century. Disputes between the priesthood and the laity occurred, sometimes because a Polish priest was removed, at other times because a Polish priest was thought to exercise too much authority. In Buffalo an entire Polish congregation was excommunicated; the members organized a new congregation, purchased land, erected a building, and declared their independence of the ecclesiastical authorities.

In 1904 some 150 representatives of independent parishes (with about 20,000 constituents in five states) met in Scranton, Pennsylvania, and organized the Polish National Catholic Church, electing the Reverend Francis Hodur as bishop. He was subsequently consecrated by bishops of the National Catholic Church of the

Netherlands. The delegates adopted a constitution and ordered that all the holy rites be translated into Polish. They passed resolutions advocating fraternal co-operation with other churches.

Doctrines. The doctrines of this Church are based on the Bible, especially the New Testament, as proclaimed by the Apostles, the first four Ecumenical Councils, and the Nicene Creed. The members reject the doctrine of papal infallibility in matters of faith and morals, holding that all men have the right to interpret the word of God according to their own consciences. The official teachings thus vary considerably from Roman Catholic doctrine. In 1921 the synod of the church authorized parish priests to marry but only with the permission of the bishop and the parish.

Worship. Worship is governed by an official liturgy. The Polish language is generally used. Various feast days have been established by the plenary synod.

Organization. There are three orders of the ministry: deacons, priests, and bishops. Each congregation is governed by a board of trustees elected by the membership. The synod consists of bishops and clerical and lay members of the local congregations. Bishops are elected by the clergy and lay members of the synod. The bishop appoints the ministers in charge of congregations after conferring with the local unit. Bishops have administrative powers, in consultation with a grand council consisting of three clerical and three lay members. The highest authority is vested in the synod.

PRESBYTERIANS

Presbyterians came to the colonies of Virginia, New England, Maryland, and Delaware from Great Britain at an early date, bringing with them the ideas of John Calvin and John Knox. The pastors of these small groups were ministers of the Church of England who held Presbyterian views. The first of these congregations was that led by the Reverend Alexander Whitaker in Virginia in 1611. Shortly thereafter one was established in Massachusetts by the Reverend Richard Denton, its worshipers coming from a church he had previously served in Yorkshire. Other pioneering churches included those in Southhold (1640) and in Jamaica (1656), both on Long Island, N.Y.

In 1683 the Presbytery of Laggan, Ireland, sent the Reverend

Francis Makemie to Maryland and Virginia in response to calls for aid. He became the apostle who brought unity to the scattered Presbyterians. The first American Presbytery was formed in Philadelphia in 1706. The first General Assembly of the Presbyterians was held in the same city in 1789.

This body, the Presbyterian Church in the United States of America, was the parent body of the Presbyterian churches in the nation. (It merged in 1958 with the United Presbyterian Church of North America to form The United Presbyterian Church in the U.S.A., the largest group of the denomination.) The Cumberland Presbyterian Church separated from it in 1810, and the Presbyterian Church in the United States (originally "in the Confederate States of America") seceded in 1861.

John Calvin (1509–1564), born in Noyon, France, was trained for the law and for the Roman Catholic priesthood. He became a partisan of the Reformation in 1533, fleeing the following year to Switzerland, where he was active as a powerful writer, an administrator of church and state, and a founder of a theology and a system of church government. Calvin's doctrines were stern. He proclaimed that the redemption of man requires regeneration by the power of the spirit of God "in the souls of the elect and of them alone." The "elect" were chosen by God to be saved; others were eternally lost (predestination).

John Knox (1505?–1572), the Scottish reformer, met Calvin in Switzerland and became the founder of Presbyterianism in his native land. His "tongue and mighty voice" evoked ardent zeal. "Rarely has any country produced a stronger will," has been said of John Knox. He relied on John 17 as the scriptural basis for his belief in election, special grace, and assured salvation. From Britain came the founders of American Presbyterianism, as noted above.

Doctrines. The teachings of Calvin and Knox have often been reinterpreted and elaborated. In the United States, Presbyterians generally hold to the principles of the undivided sovereignty of God in the universe He created, the sovereignty of Christ in salvation, the sovereignty of the Scriptures in matters of faith and conduct, and the sovereignty of the individual conscience in scriptural interpretation. The Westminister Confession of Faith, prepared by an assembly appointed by the English Puritan Parliament (1643), is the general creed of English-speaking Presbyterians. The sacraments of the Lord's Supper and of baptism are recognized.

Worship. Presbyterian bodies may have their official order of worship for use in local congregations, though there is no restriction on the form or order of the local service. Ministers and congregations are authorized to worship with freedom of conscience. Several of the smaller American bodies founded by immigrants from Scotland prescribe the exclusive use of the Psalms for congregational singing.

Organization. The Presbyterian system of church government is shared with the group of churches called Reformed (see below). Church authority is vested in representative bodies rather than individuals. The chief bodies are: the local church session, consisting of the ministers and the ruling presbyters, or elders (elected lay representatives), which governs the congregation; the Presbytery, an association of a group of churches in a geographical district, which governs the local churches; the Synod, a representative body that governs the congregations over a larger area than the Presbytery, often an entire state; and the General Assembly, which is the supreme representative and governing body. Ministers are ordained by the Presbyteries. The session of the local church examines individuals who apply for church membership. Administrative boards are in charge of educational activities and missionary work at home and abroad.

PROTESTANTISM

Many religious denominations in the United States are classified as Protestant. These groups or families of religious bodies are described in this volume, as are other individual bodies with 100,000 members or more, and a few smaller denominations whose histories are somewhat distinctive. The following account recapitulates basic characteristics of Protestantism.

Protestantism is one of the three major branches of Christendom, the others being the Eastern Orthodox Church and the Roman Catholic Church. Its origins are usually dated from October 31, 1517, when the Augustinian monk Martin Luther nailed his famous Ninety-five Theses to the door of the castle church in Wittenberg, Germany. (See Lutherans.) Luther was accused of heresy, excommunicated by the Pope, and tried at the Diet of Worms (an assembly of the Holy Roman Empire). There he remained firm, while some German princes and electors resisted the Diet's sentence placing Luther under the ban of the Empire. As Luther left Worms, friends conducted him to the safety of the Castle of the Wartburg in Thuringia. There he began his translation of the Bible into German, completing it ten years later.

Soon Martin Luther was at the center of a great schism, the beneficiary of economic, political, and religious forces and movements. Many German secular rulers were ready to throw off ecclesiastical control. Intellectuals were in revolt against the scholasticism of Catholic philosophy. Although there had been Protestant groups before Luther (see Moravians), he became the leader of the major forces of the Reformation. His was such a powerful voice that the entire period of the Reformation is generally associated with his declarations and labors.

Luther and his early associates in Germany were conservatives in doctrine. A modification of Roman Catholic liturgy was devised, and the authority of the Bible was affirmed: Every man should read it and *protest* (meaning "bear witness to") his private judgment, for which he was responsible directly to God. This doctrine gave rise to difficulties: there were all sorts of judgments. There would be a priesthood of all believers, the minister being only the first among equals—a standard that was not universally observed or approximated. Protestants have emphasized religious liberty, not always consistently, but with considerable force, throughout the world.

Most Protestants affirm that God is triune, confessing Him in the familiar words: "Father, Son, and Holy Spirit." The exceptions are the Unitarians, who believe in the strict humanity of Jesus. Thus, most Protestants are called Trinitarians. They generally believe that God deals with man primarily through grace rather than through law. They do not approve of faith without works—man should do good works to express his gratitude to God. Furthermore, man should give freely of his means as a sign of his thanks to God for His goodness and mercy. Protestants believe in the eternal life with God, and in the Church as a fellowship of the believers in and followers of Christ.

Two broad changes evolved during the first century of Protestantism.

One development was the spread of "protests against Protestantism." These liberalizing intellectual and social movements gave rise to bodies far different from the Lutheranism of Germany: Friends, Brethren, Mennonites, Baptists, Unitarians, and Universalists.

A second broad development, unrelated to the first, arose within the Church of England. Beginning in 1833, several powerful personalities associated with Oxford University—Edward B. Pusey, John Keble, and John Henry (later Cardinal) Newman—started what is still called the Oxford Movement, or Anglo-Catholicism, or the High Church party in the Anglican Communion. This movement emphasizes Catholic tradition and endeavors to recover essential elements of the undivided Church prior to the schism of East and West in 1054, but it does not acknowledge the distinctive Roman claims of the primacy of the Pope. Members of this party, found in considerable numbers in the Protestant Episcopal Church in the United States and within Anglicanism in other countries, call themselves "Catholic."

Throughout the world, and in the United States in particular, it has often been said that the "essence of Protestantism is division." There is evidence of all sorts to support this generalization. There are more denominations than ever before in the United States. Still, two counterdevelopments have begun to share the scene with the divisive tendencies. These are:

(1) Inter-Protestant co-operation, largely in the form of many councils of churches—local, state, national, and international. These activities are often included in the over-all term, Ecumenical Movement, defined as a world-wide effort to achieve co-operation that emphasizes common interests. The Eastern Churches also participate in this movement.

(2) Organic unions of mergers of churches, which have been significant in the United States and elsewhere. (Important newly formed bodies in the United States are listed on pp. 84–85.) Notable examples in other nations are the United Church of Canada (1925), a merger of the Congregational, Methodist, and some of the Presbyterian churches of that country; the Church of South India (1947), uniting the Anglican, Congregational, Methodist, Presbyterian, and Reformed bodies; and the Church of Christ in Japan (1941), uniting fifteen Protestant bodies.

PROTESTANT EPISCOPAL CHURCH (EPISCOPAL CHURCH)

The Protestant Episcopal Church in the United States is one of the eighteen independent religious bodies that grew out of the Church of England as it expanded during the great age of British discovery and commerce. In America this church established its first place of worship at Jamestown, Virginia, in 1607. A separate national church body was formed in the United States in 1789. The principal characteristics of the Protestant Episcopal Church have thus been derived from the Church of England, which in 1534, after a long process of separation, became independent of the Roman Catholic Church. In that year King Henry VIII secured for himself "the headship" of the church, and the Church of England (in contrast to later Anglican churches) became an established or state church. The eighteen national churches of the Anglican Communion are bound together by common traditions of faith, form of worship, and church order. The bishops of all these churches meet once every ten years in the Lambeth Conference, London, for consultation.

Doctrines. Two of the three historic Christian creeds express for American Episcopalians their sense of the Scriptures and constitute the symbols of their faith. These are the Apostles' Creed and the Nicene Creed. The American Convention of 1789 rejected the Athanasian Creed, which is accepted by other bodies in the Anglican Communion. The Apostles' Creed, once called "the old Roman symbol," is accepted by many Protestant bodies throughout the world and by the Roman Catholic Church. It was in use in its present form at about A.D. 650. The Nicene Creed is named after the Council of Nicea (A.D. 324), although there is good evidence that it was written much earlier by St. Cyril in Jerusalem. The Council of Constantinople (A.D. 381) introduced revisions that cast it in its present form. Two of the differences between the Apostles' Creed and the Nicene Creed are that the Apostles' Creed refers to "resurrection of the body" whereas the Nicene Creed reads "resurrection of the dead," and that the words "He descended into hell" appear in the Apostles' Creed, but are omitted in the Nicene Creed.

The articles of religion of the Church of England were accepted with modifications by the American Episcopal Convention of 1789. These Thirty-nine Articles, dating from the reign of Queen Elizabeth I, are understood to deal with matters less significant than those of the Apostles' and Nicene Creeds. Written by a group of bishops who were influenced by Calvinistic theology (see Presbyterians), they repudiate the Roman Catholic concept of purgatory and certain other teachings of that Church. They also affirm that Christ established only two sacraments: baptism and the Lord's Supper.

The Episcopalian catechism contains instruction in history, worship, and doctrine for persons preparing to appear before a bishop for confirmation. In this Church, only a bishop can confirm. Baptism of children as well as of adults is by pouring or by immersion in water.

As in some other religious bodies, there are three distinct parties or schools of thought: a High Church or Anglo-Catholic group, originating for the most part in the Oxford Movement in England during the first half of the nineteenth century, which emphasizes restoration of certain Roman Catholic traditions, but not the primacy of the Pope; a Low Church party, which stresses evangelical or generally Protestant traditions; and with a point of view midway between the two, a group of broad-minded churchmen, some of whom are often referred to as liberals or rationalists.

Although formally organized in 1789, the year in which the Federal Government was established, the Protestant Episcopal Church grew but slowly during the succeeding fifty years. This lag has been attributed in large part to anti-British feeling that prevailed among the American people. The Episcopal Church went West with the pioneers, and it maintained its unity in spite of the strains of the Civil War. Soon it entered upon the same broad programs of home and foreign missions, education, evangelism, and social welfare that are carried on by all the nation's large religious bodies.

Worship. The Church is liturgical in its form of worship. Its Book of Common Prayer contains the orders for morning prayer, evening prayer, the litany, and the Holy Communion, which "are the regular services appointed for public worship in this church, and shall be used accordingly." Subject to ecclesiastical approval, the minister may use "other devotions" described in the Book of Common Prayer "when edification of the congregation so requires, in place of the order for morning prayer, or the order for evening prayer."

Organization. The officers of a parish are a rector (priest), and elected lay wardens (usually two) and vestrymen—the latter being trustees of the property. Dioceses, often following state lines, are governed by a convention of the parish clergy and at least one lay delegate from each parish. The diocesan conventions elect the bishops, who are the administrators of the Church activities. The General Convention, meeting every three years, consists of elected clergy and lay delegates. It is organized in much the same way as the Congress of the United States, with a House of Deputies and a House of Bishops. The head of the Church is the Presiding Bishop, who is elected by the General Convention. A National Council, established in 1919, carries on the work of the body between sessions of the General Convention.

There are three orders in the ministry: deacons, priests, and bishops. A deacon who has served in the ministry for one year and is twenty-four years of age or older may be ordained to the priesthood. To become a bishop a priest must be elected to the office by a diocesan convention, subject to approval by a majority of the bishops of the United States and of the standing committees of the dioceses.

QUAKERS

(See FRIENDS)

REFORMED CHURCHES

During the Protestant Reformation, a large group of churches diverging from the German Lutheran tradition arose in Switzerland, the Netherlands, and Germany under the leadership of Huldreich Zwingli (1483–1531), Philip Melanchthon (1497–1560), and John Calvin (1509–1564). These were the Reformed Churches. In Scotland and other parts of Britain similar groups became known as Presbyterians (which see).

In New Amsterdam in 1628, in Fort Orange (now Albany) in 1642, and in Newcastle, Delaware, in 1650, settlers from the Netherlands formed small congregations of what is now the Reformed Church in America. The congregation in New York City, the Collegiate Church, is believed to be the oldest local church in the Middle Atlantic States. At first, work in America was under jurisdiction of the Classis of Amsterdam, but steps were taken, beginning in 1747, to form an independent American body. The first General Synod of the Reformed Church in America was organized in 1792.

The present-day Christian Reformed Church was organized in 1846–47 in Michigan and Iowa by immigrants from the Netherlands who were interested in building a church life of their own. One center (Holland) in Michigan and another (Pella) in Iowa were part of the Reformed Church. They separated from the Reformed Church in 1857 and organized a denomination of their own, adopting the name of Christian Reformed Church in 1890. (See also United Church of Christ.)

Doctrines. The historic doctrines of the Reformed Churches are summarized in three documents: the Belgic Confession of Faith (1561), the Heidelberg Catechism (1563), and the Canons of the Synod of Dort (1619). Their theological emphasis is Calvinist in origin. These confessions of faith all stress salvation through Christ as their central theme. They affirm the primacy of God and His power in the affairs of men, and the final authority of the Scriptures as the living word of God, available to all men through the Holy Spirit.

Worship. The form of worship is "semiliturgical" in the Reformed Churches. The order may be modified considerably at ordinary Sunday services. Prescribed orders of worship are set forth for the Lord's Supper, baptism, and the ordination of ministers. Forms of prayer and of marriage services are optional. Adherents of the Reformed Churches claim that they have a blending of form and freedom in their worship.

Organization. The form of government is Presbyterian, though some of the terminology differs (e.g., *classis* instead of *presbytery*). The members of a local church elect a consistory, consisting of the minister, elders, and deacons to govern the congregation. The Classis is an association of representatives of the local churches, which supervises these churches and their ministers. The General

Synod consists of ministers and elders elected from the Classes by representative voting. It is the highest court and administrative body of the denomination.

ROMAN CATHOLICS

The first Reformed Catholic community in the United States was established in St. Augustine, Florida, in 1565, although worship had been conducted previously at various other places in Florida. From St. Augustine missionaries traveled along the coast, preaching to the Indians. The year 1565 is also considered to mark the beginning of systematic evangelizing in Latin America by Roman Catholics.

Missionaries had accompanied Coronado's expedition into what is now New Mexico in 1540. On the Pacific Coast, Franciscans were active as missionaries from about 1600. Priests from France conducted services on the coast of Maine in 1609 and on Mount Desert Island in 1612. Jesuit missions were first established on the upper Kennebec River in 1646. In 1665 Catholic missionaries, who had preached on the shores of the Great Lakes as early as 1641, endeavored to convert the Onondaga Indians and other tribes.

In the British colony of Maryland, founded by refugee Catholics, parishes were established at St. Mary's in 1634, at St. Ingoes in 1638, at Kent Island in 1639, at Port Tobacco in 1641, and at Patuxent in 1647. Severe restrictions were imposed on Roman Catholics in most of the other colonies. By 1700 there were only a few Catholic families in New York, for example, although by 1763 Maryland had twelve Catholic missionaries with some sixteen thousand of the faithful, and neighboring Pennsylvania had five missionaries and over five thousand worshipers.

At the end of the Revolutionary War, Catholics in the former colonies were without any ecclesiastical supervision. In 1784, however, the Reverend John Carroll was appointed prefect-apostolic for the Catholics of the former thirteen colonies. Father Carroll was appointed bishop for the United States in 1789, with Baltimore as his see.

The Holy Catholic and Apostlic Roman Church, to give it its official title, recognizes the Bishop of Rome, the Pope, as the Vicar of Christ on earth and as the head of the Church. It traces its origin to the commission given by Christ to Peter, "prince of the apostles" (based on Matthew 16:18–19). The authority of Peter as head of the early Apostolic Church is believed to be exercised by his successors as the Bishops of Rome.

Doctrines. The Roman Catholic Church, the largest body in Christendom, regards the Apostles' Creed, the Nicene Creed, and the Athanasian Creed as containing the essential truths accepted by the Church. It holds that these doctrines are more fully stated in the deposit of faith given by Christ through His Apostles. That deposit is sustained by the Holy Scriptures and by tradition. These doctrines are defined and safeguarded by the Pope when he speaks as head of the Church on matters of faith and morals.

A person joining the Roman Catholic Church is required to assent to a formulation of doctrine in the following "profession of faith":

"One only God, in three divine persons, distinct from and equal to, each other—that is to say, the Father, the Son, and the Holy Ghost.

"The Catholic doctrine of the Incarnation, Passion, Death, and Resurrection of our Lord Jesus Christ; and the personal union of the two natures, the divine and the human; the divine maternity of the Most Holy Mary, together with her most spotless virginity.

"The true, real, and substantial presence of the Body and Blood, together with the Soul and Divinity of our Lord Jesus Christ, in the most holy Sacrament of the Eucharist.

"The seven sacraments instituted by Jesus Christ for the salvation of mankind, that is to say: Baptism, Confirmation, Eucharist, Penance, Extreme Unction, Orders, Matrimony.

"Purgatory, the resurrection of the dead, everlasting life.

"The primacy, not only of honor, but also of jurisdiction, of the Roman Pontiff, successor of St. Peter, Prince of the Apostles, Vicar of Jesus Christ; the veneration of the saints and of their images; the authority of the apostolic and ecclesiastical traditions; and of the Holy Scriptures, which we must interpret and understand, only in the sense which our Holy Mother the Catholic Church has held and does hold; and everything else that has been defined and declared by the sacred canons, and by the General Councils, and particularly by the Holy Council of Trent, and delivered, defined, and declared by the General Council of the Vatican, especially concerning the primacy of the Roman Pontiff, and his infallible teaching authority."

Baptism is performed by pouring of water for infants as well as adults. This ceremony together with repetition of the proper words by a priest "cleanses from original sin." Baptism is a condition of membership in the Church, whether the sacrament be administered to infants or to adults. Upon his baptism, the name of a person is officially registered as a Catholic on the parish records and is so retained unless he renounces membership by a formal act or is formally excommunicated from the Church.

The chief requirements prescribed by the Church for its members are: to attend Mass on Sundays and Holy Days of obligation; to fast and abstain on the days appointed; to confess at least once a year; to receive the Holy Eucharist at Easter; to contribute to the support of pastors; and to observe the regulations governing marriage.

Worship. The form of worship follows a prescribed liturgy. Mass is celebrated every day in a parish church. Sunday Masses are offered in the local churches, the High Mass being the one usually celebrated between 10:00 A.M. and noon. Masses are offered in the parishes as often as needed by the parishoners. At High Mass most of the priest's prayers are chanted, and the responses are sung by a choir. At Low Mass the service is read; prior to 1964 (see p. 68) there was brief instruction by the priest instead of a sermon. Vespers are sometimes sung on Sunday afternoons or evenings. Roman Catholic churches are usually kept open all day for prayer. The liturgy was formerly required to be in Latin, except for one group of churches, the "Uniate," which were permitted to use ancient forms of their old languages. (The Uniate churches originated in countries of the Middle East, but later a number of them were organized by immigrants to other countries, including the United States.) A ruling of Vatican II (see p. 68), however, permitted some use of the vernacular (the native language of a country) instead of Latin. In all Roman Catholic churches the sermons, the instructions, and the readings of the Scriptures are in the vernacular of the congregation.

Far-reaching reforms in the liturgy for Holy Week (the week before Easter) were decreed by Pope Pius XII, effective in 1956. They were designed to enlarge the participation of the laity and to restore ancient beauty and solemnity. The holding of some services in the afternoon and evening hours was authorized in order to enable more people to attend. All members, both clergy and laity, may receive communion on Good Friday.

Organization. The form of organization of the Roman Catholic Church is that of a hierarchy. The Pope is supreme, both in matters of faith and in administrative policy. The administrative body through which he governs is called the Curia Romana. Next in rank to the Pope is the College of Cardinals; some cardinals as bishops administer important archdioceses abroad, while those who live in Rome administer the numerous agencies of the Vatican (called Congregations) which form part of the Curia Romana. When a Pope dies, the College of Cardinals temporarily holds supreme authority and elects a new Pope.

In the United States, the organization consists of an Apostolic Delegate appointed by the Pope; the American cardinals; the archbishops and bishops in charge of archdioceses and dioceses, respectively; the priests in charge of parishes; and the faithful laity. The bishop, appointed by the Pope, ordains priests and appoints them to parishes. The priest, who is subject to the bishop, administers the sacraments, conducts worship, and is responsible for the affairs of the parish. The laity are consulted about secular management of the parish, but have no voice in the selection of the parish priest. The cash salary of the priest is fixed by each diocese and is uniform within the diocesan boundaries. The dioceses generally cover areas smaller than the various states in which they are situated.

Much of the church work is done by the numerous religious orders. The orders consist of (1) religious congregations of priests (some of which have unordained members who take care of ordinary business), and (2) brotherhoods and sisterhoods. The so-called "regular" priests are members of congregations who live under the rule of a religious order, although they are ordained and may be appointed by a bishop in the same manner as the other ("diocesan" or "secular") clergy. Members of brotherhoods and sisterhoods take vows, but they are not ordained. Most of them concentrate on educational work or social welfare activities. They are spiritually under the jurisdiction of the bishop, but are assigned to their tasks and positions by the superiors of their orders.

Most of the colleges and universities controlled by the Roman Catholic Church are under the supervision of the various religious orders. The great majority of parishes have elementary parochial schools, in which sisters do the teaching. Parochial high schools in the dioceses admit a considerable number of elementary parochial school graduates. The religious orders have played a prominent part in all these educational programs. In addition, local parishes are required to offer religious instruction for Catholic children who attend public schools; this instruction is provided either weekdays or on Sunday as convenient.

The Catholic charities in the dioceses are well organized for the support of institutions for children and for the aged and of numerous general hospitals. These are National Councils (of Catholic Men, of Catholic Women, and of Catholic Youth) under the direction of the National Catholic Welfare Conference, which is an organization of the bishops of the United States for promoting unity in Catholic work.

The Roman Catholic Church of the United States is the fourth largest of its kind in the world, being outnumbered only by the Catholic churches of Brazil, Italy, and France.

Vatican II * (the Twenty-first Ecumenical Council) convened by the late Pope John XXIII in 1962 and reconvened by Pope Paul VI in 1963, has received much attention in the United States from Catholics and from members of other religious denominations. The appointment of a Secretariat of Christian Unity by Pope John XXIII as part of the Council preparations, and the presence at the Council of some forty delegate-observers from other Christian denominations at the invitation of the Secretariat were actions that made for new understanding between Roman Catholics and other Christian churches. Pope John XXIII was widely known and admired by non-Catholics, and his influence was felt by many people in the United States and other countries. Two of his Encyclicals, *Christianity and Social Progress* (1961) and *Peace on Earth* (1963), were read and appreciated in many circles outside the Roman Catholic Church.

The 1963 session of Vatican II made decisions leading to important changes, several of which are here noted. The sacrament of extreme unction was renamed "the anointing of the sick." The preaching of a sermon at every Mass was made mandatory, effective early in 1964. The Council granted discretionary power to a

* So called because it is the second Council to be held in St. Peter's Basilica in the Vatican.

bishop, or collectively to the bishops of a nation or territory, to use the vernacular instead of Latin in the Mass and in the administration of the sacraments, with the proviso that the Pope approve the changes. The bishops of the United States announced in 1964 that they had made arrangements for a translation, which, after being approved by the Pope, is already in use. This is a tentative or preliminary version. More than half of the text is in English, the other portion remaining in Latin. Approved English text for administration of the sacraments, except for Holy Orders, is also available.

The 1964 session favored granting discretionary authority to a bishop to permit Roman Catholics, in special circumstances, to participate in common worship with Protestants, a policy previously strictly opposed by the Church.

SALVATION ARMY

William Booth (1829–1912), an English Methodist minister, traveled through the streets of London's East End in 1865; he was so affected by what he saw that upon his return home he told his wife that he had found his mission in life. They immediately devoted themselves to the task of seeking out lost humanity and aiding in their salvation. Booth organized the East London Mission, preaching in the streets, and later moving to a tent. Many in the East End heard him, and as he sought to penetrate the gross darkness with the light of Christ's message, many "moral miracles" occurred in the lives of his listeners.

Soon missions were established in other British cities, all under the informal guidance of William Booth, who was regarded as their general superintendent. A conference of representatives from local missions was held annually. In his report to the Conference of 1878, Booth stated: "The Christian Mission is a volunteer army." The associates to whom he read this line suggested he delete the word "volunteer." Booth crossed out "volunteer" and substituted "salvation." His report to the Conference was well received, and the "Salvation Army" was acclaimed. The missionaries became known as captains, the members as soldiers, and the general superintendent as the general. The movement's magazine was named "War Cry." Then the crusaders set out across the seas, first to the

United States in 1880, when a branch was established in Pennsylvania, and later to most of the other nations of the world.

Doctrines. The doctrines of the Salvation Army are orthodox trinitarian. They emphasize a holy God, a holy Bible, and a holy people. Holiness of life is a demand made upon the adherents: a right life is the foundation of all effective service. The members affirm that they have willingly surrendered themselves to God. In general, the doctrines are warmly "Arminian" rather than "Calvinist," holding that the love of God is as wide as His universe, and that He gives His gifts freely to all.

Members are sought not only among the less fortunate in society, but from all walks of life. The Salvation Army operates hostels and workshops for the rehabilitation of the needy. The officers give material relief and counseling as well as understanding and sympathy to the neglected and the handicapped.

Worship. Worship is altogether informal and often held out-of-doors. It consists of hymns, prayers, the reading of Scripture, offerings, and preaching, all in the order preferred by the local branch.

Organization. The local unit of the Salvation Army is the corps. Large cities may have numerous corps. Anyone converted to Christ and favoring the Salvation Army's way of life may apply as a recruit and be "sworn in." Once in the corps, the member may become a candidate for the rank of officer. As noted above, the over-all form of government is military.

SMALL SECTS

Some three hundred of the small religious groups commonly referred to as *sects* have been identified and classified. Sects are comparatively small religious bodies with fairly rigid or complete discipline and control of their members. These bodies are organized into congregations, usually with frequent personal contacts among members and between pastor and congregation.*

The small sects are much alike in their point of view (as expo-

* Many of the sects were not included in the various census of religious bodies and are not reported in the annual *Yearbook of American Churches.* E. T. Clark devoted twenty-five years to a study of these bodies, which he described in his *The Small Sects in America* (Nashville, Tenn.: Abingdon Press, 1949).

nents of a Puritan morality and theological conservatism) and in their functions as refuges for the poor and as centers of human relations for lonely people. In these groups, however, we find "religion as it springs naturally from the naive and simple heart that craves touch with the supernatural, and is unaffected by the conventions and the scientific learnings of a sophisticated society."

Included among small sects are the following types of religious bodies: Adventist *; Perfectionist or Subjectivist, such as Nazarenes * and Holiness * bodies; Charismatic or Pentecostal *; and Legalistic, such as Mennonites,* Brethren,* and some of the Baptist * bodies.

UNITARIANS AND UNIVERSALISTS

A new religious body, the Unitarian Universalist Association, was formed in 1961 by merger of the Unitarian Churches with the Universalist Church of America. (The merging groups had been founded late in the eighteenth century: in 1780 the Universalists established their first church—in Gloucester, Masschusetts; and in 1782 King's Chapel in Boston became the first local congregation to accept the Unitarian faith formally.)

Doctrines. The Unitarian doctrine of the strict humanity of Jesus (opposed to the trinitarian belief) has attracted adherents throughout many centuries of Christian history. In fact, the modern Unitarian movement can be traced as far back as a half-century after the Protestant Reformation. It developed in England during the eighteenth century. In America the Unitarian Churches were an outgrowth of Congregationalism (see Congregationalists), although establishment of Unitarianism as a denomination was a most gradual process. From 1750 to 1800 several Congregational local churches adopted a relatively liberal position, ably interpreted by William Ellery Channing, whose eloquent sermon at Baltimore in 1819 made him an outstanding leader of the movement. In 1825 the American Unitarian Association was organized to advance the common interests of the local churches.

Universalism, holding that there is a beneficient and sane universe in which right, truth, and love are supreme and that it is

* See entries under these titles.

God's purpose to save every member of the human race, has been a point of view held by some individuals ever since the beginnings of Christianity. The Universalist Church as a denomination in America dates from about 1770, with the arrival from London of the Reverend John Murray, whose teachings stimulated widespread interest in the movement. Efforts to form a national denominational organization began as early as 1785 in Oxford, Massachusetts, and eventually succeeded at the Centennial Convention of 1870. In later years of the denomination, it became apparent that many Universalists were also Unitarians.

Organization. Neither the Unitarian Churches nor the Universalist Church had ever adopted an official creed. Their common interests were increasingly recognized, however, and in 1953 they formed the Council of Liberal Churches, which was to administer such joint projects and programs as the two bodies might assign to it. The operations of the Council of Liberal Churches eventually led to the formation of plans for uniting the two bodies, an objective achieved in 1961. The United body, the Unitarian Universalist Association, is congregational in government and does not require its local churches and members to adhere to any official doctrine. The local church also controls the form of worship.

UNITED CHURCH OF CHRIST

The United Church of Christ is a union, effected in 1961, of the Congregational Christian Churches with the Evangelical and Reformed Church, which, similarly, was established in 1934 through merger of the Reformed Church in the United States with the Evangelical Synod of North America.

The first Congregational churches were established in Massachusetts: at Plymouth in 1620, at Salem in 1629, and at Boston in 1630 (see Congregationalists). The Reformed Church in the United States traces its origin to the formal organization of a local group in 1725 at Falkner Swamp (north of Philadelphia), although there had been a few sporadic units elsewhere in the colonies. In 1840 six ministers met at Gravois Settlement, Missouri, to form an association of then independent Lutheran and Reformed congregations which later became the Evangelical Synod of North America.

Discussion of ways and means of forming the United Church of Christ began in 1942, nearly twenty years before the final step of adopting a constitution was taken. Most of the opposition came from Congregational circles. An inquiry in 1948 among Congregational churches had indicated that 75 per cent would favor a merger. The opponents were concerned that some of the traditional freedom from external authority enjoyed by the local church might be endangered. Union was partially effected in 1957, but further progress was halted temporarily by an unsuccessful lawsuit brought by a congregation in Brooklyn. In 1961, about 72 per cent of the local Congregational churches approved the merger. It became clear, however, that many of the members opposing the merger had failed to vote; and, in fact, two associations of dissenting Congregational churches have been established.

Proponents of unity spoke glowingly of a step "away from the scandal of denominationalism" and "toward that one world which the church should at once prophesy and demonstrate." They were convinced that the merger was "the will of God." "This," said one of its advocates, "is probably the most important step our churches have been called to take, or will be called to take, in this century."

Doctrine. The United Church of Christ prescribes no specific doctrinal standards nor forms of worship for members of local churches. Its Constitution broadly states that the United Church "claims as its own the faith expressed in the ancient creeds and reclaimed in the basic insights of the Protestant Reformation. It affirms the responsibility of the church in each generation to make this faith its own in reality of worship, in honesty of thought and expression, and in purity of heart before God."

A "testimony, not a test," was adopted by the General Synod in 1959, as follows:

"We believe in God, the Eternal Spirit, Father of our Lord Jesus Christ and our Father, to whose deeds we testify:

"He calls the worlds into being, creates man in His own image, and sets before him the ways of life and death.

"He seeks in holy love to save all people from aimlessness and sin.

"He judges men and nations by His righteous will declared through prophets and apostles.

"In Jesus Christ, the man of Nazareth, our crucified and risen

Lord, He has come to us and shared our common lot, conquering sin and death and reconciling the world to Himself.

"He bestows upon us His Holy Spirit, creating and renewing the Church of Jesus Christ, binding in covenant faithful people of all ages, tongues, and races.

"He calls us into His church to accept the cost and joy of discipleship, to be His servants in the service of men, to proclaim the Gospel to all the world and resist the powers of evil, to share in Christ's baptism and eat at His table, to join Him in His passion and victory.

"He promises to all who trust Him forgiveness of sins and fulness of grace, courage in the struggle for justice and peace, His presence in trial and rejoicing, and eternal life in His kingdom which has no end.

"Blessing and honor, glory and power be unto Him. Amen."

Worship and Organization. The union was acclaimed as the first merger of churches differing widely in cultural background: the "Separatist" Congregationalists of English origin and the Evangelical and Reformed groups of German origin. They had differed also in organization, for the Evangelical and Reformed Church adopted the presbyterian system (see Presbyterians), although it employed its own terminology—e.g., using the term *classis* instead of *presbytery,* whereas the Congregationalists, as their name implied, were devoted to the autonomy of the local congregation. The present united group is regarded as congregational both in worship and in organization. Its constitution set forth this basic policy: "Nothing in this constitution . . . shall be construed as giving to the General Synod, or to any conference or Association, now or at any time, power to abridge or impair the autonomy of any local church. . . ."

VEDANTA

Vedanta may be described as a branch of Hinduism (or as a movement within the world religion of Hinduism); it was founded in India during the 1890's by Ramakrishna Paramahansa, a seer and mystic who sought the unity of all religions because he believed that all have the same ultimate goal. In 1893, one of his followers, Swami Vivekananda, made an impressive address at the Parliament of Religions held at the Chicago World's Fair. Vivekananda soon became the first teacher of Vedanta in the West, starting a Vedanta Society in New York. There are now twelve centers in large cities of the United States, under the general direction of the Ramakrishna Order of India, in Belur, Calcutta.

Doctrines. Vedanta asserts that man is potentially divine and that the purpose of his life is to realize this truth through prayer, meditation, spiritual inquiry, and unselfish work. It emphasizes the spiritual transformation of human lives. Its adherents believe that they represent the essence of all religions, recognizing the same divine inspiration in all.

Worship. Sunday services include lectures, readings, and meditations. Classes are also held for studying the religious literature of India, including the Upanishads, the Bhagavad-Gita, the writing of a leader named Shankara, and the Patanjoli aphorisms. Two of the American centers have monasteries and convents. In all centers the dual emphasis is upon social service and education.

Organization. The local centers are independent and self-supporting, most of them with boards of trustees consisting of United States citizens. Religious leaders sent to the United States by the Ramakrishna Order of India serve as "guest teachers," not as missionaries. (In India there are about two hundred Vedanta centers, with associated hospitals, dispensaries, high schools, trade and agricultural schools, libraries, publishing houses, and a university. The Order has been particularly active in assisting victims of floods, famines, earthquakes, and epidemics.)

YOGA

Yoga is a way of living that is strictly followed by some Hindu groups but is not restricted to them. It is an attitude of mind, a point of view or conviction, founded upon the ideal of attaining union with god—the common aim of mystics in all religious bodies. It is a method of freeing the spirit of man, thus giving him access to the great and creative powers of the universe. In practice the chief emphasis is often placed upon "thought control" as a means of developing extraordinary power over the human physique. For a devout follower of the method, many years of exercise, meditation, and devotion are required. These exercises, together with extremely simple personal habits and "a single heart," lead the soul into a state of illumination.

ZEN BUDDHISM

Zen Buddhism is a school of thought within Buddhism. It originated in India in the sixth century and later spread to China and Japan. Adherents of Zen have been active in the United States since 1900 and, from time to time, have formed small, informal groups recruited largely among intellectuals in a few large cities.

Followers of Zen practice highly disciplined meditation in order to attain enlightenment. This process is a mystical one; sometimes the disciple has a "master" and may interrupt a long period of meditation to consult his mentor, who often uses paradoxes and surprises to bring him to awareness. An authority on Zen writes of intellectual power as a "taint." Zen cannot be fully grasped or described, or adequately known. There is no formulated creed, no organized litany, no formal congregation, all of which are regarded as useless for attaining enlightenment. In the United States this authentic Zen has attracted very few adherents.

Out of authentic Zen has come "Beat Zen," whose followers are alienated from (or in revolt against) American culture. Adherents of Beat Zen have borrowed certain ideas from authentic Zen and have misinterpreted or misapplied them. They gather informally in small groups in the large cities; many of them are so-called "beatniks," certain that their point of view is unique, that they are the first genuinely total rebels against established American ways, the inspired devotees of a voluntary society.

It is reported that there is also a "Square Zen" in the United States, marked by extreme respectability, in contrast to Beat Zen. "Square Zen" is likewise regarded as a departure from authentic Zen. (See Buddhism, Vedanta, and Yoga.)

PART TWO

QUICK-REFERENCE GUIDE

This section summarizes briefly some of the outstanding features, problems, and trends among contemporary American religious groups. The topics, arranged in alphabetical order, are those most widely discussed and of the greatest interest both to religious leaders and to general readers.

American Religions. The principal religious groups in America owing their origins to European, Oriental, or other immigrants are listed below. (Since their formation, many of them have undergone division, union, or reorganization. The tendency of such groups to vary somewhat from the traditional forms customary in the mother countries has helped to make them distinctively American institutions.)

- Bahá'í
- Baptists
- Brethren, German Baptist
- Buddhists
- Churches of the New Jerusalem (Swedenborgian)
- Congregationalists
- Eastern Orthodox groups
- Episcopalians (in the Protestant Episcopal Church)
- Friends
- Jewish Congregations
- Lutherans
- Mennonites
- Methodists
- Moravians
- Muslims
- Old Catholics
- Plymouth Brethren
- Presbyterians
- Reformed Churches
- Roman Catholics
- Salvation Army
- Vedanta (Hindu)
- Yoga
- Zen (several types)

The principal indigenous American religious movements resulting in formation of new denominations may be indicated as follows:

- Adventists
- Christian and Missionary Alliance
- Christian Science (Church of Christ, Scientist)
- Churches of Christ
- Churches of God
- Disciples of Christ
- Ethical Culture
- Evangelistic Associations

Federated Churches
Fundamentalist Churches
Holiness Bodies
Independent or Undenominational Churches
Indians' Religious Institutions
Informal Religious Fellowships
International Church of the Four-Square Gospel
Jehovah's Witnesses
Latter-Day Saints
Nazarenes
Pentecostal Bodies
Polish National Catholic Church
Small Sects
Unitarians and Universalists
United Church of Christ (Congregational Christian Churches and Evangelical and Reformed Church)

Basic Beliefs Held in Common. It may be said that adherents of the four main religions in the United States agree upon the following fundamental beliefs. (These are obviously not complete statements of the beliefs of Judaism, Roman Catholicism, Eastern Orthodoxy, or Protestantism. Furthermore, some readers may take exception to certain interpretations below, and perhaps rightly, for these simplified generalizations invite qualification, elaboration, or exception.)

General Beliefs of Four Denominations. The following are broad principles to which the adherents of the four mass religions ascribe:

They believe in one God, Creator and Sustainer of the universe, whom they worship. They give allegiance to Him and they acknowledge that this allegiance is their highest.

They believe that they are the object of the love and grace of God, and that they are called upon to declare his glory and power.

They hold that God manifests Himself through His wondrous works, including especially the mind, will, and heart of man. They believe that the mind of man may reflect, though imperfectly, the mind of God. Consequently, all minds of all men share in a basic equality through their divine inspiration. Equality is accompanied by ideals of justice, peace, mutual respect, humility, mercy, and forgiveness.

Though divided in outward forms, they often express unity both in spirit and in good works. Though they may differently understand God's purposes for them, they believe that a deeper understanding will eventually lead them to a more united apprehension of God's truth. They are thankful that in recent times they have often been drawn together and that consequently some misunderstandings have been removed. They pray that God will guide them to a greater unity. Though worshiping in separate buildings, they have often lifted their hearts together in prayer. They rejoice that they all use one book of Scriptures in common—the Scriptures of the Jews, the Old Testament of the Christians.

When they meet they are able to agree, looking beyond barriers separating peoples, upon points of view and moral standards held in common. They thus often feel a deepened sense of unity. They are convinced that they must seek, under God's guidance, ways of manifesting their unities in the world. They seek to unite for the avoidance of evil and for the accomplishment of good works. They believe that every sincere attempt to co-operate among themselves in the concerns of the Kingdom of God draws separated people and organizations together in mutual understanding. They advocate such co-operation. They seek to learn from those who differ from them.

They believe that devotion to God is the great hope of the peoples of the world in their present extremities and distractions. They believe that religious principles are the basis of good social order; that these principles serve to give moral unity to society; that the good society is being built when men seek to live for each other, strive for brotherhood, and are imbued with the spirit of justice and dedicated to the discovery and teaching of truth and to the practice of wise, rational conduct.

They believe that the moral law should govern world order; that international institutions to maintain peace with justice should be organized and preserved; that the material resources of the earth have been entrusted to men by God for the benefit of all.

Specific Personal Beliefs. Certain of the more specific personal beliefs common to the four main religions in the United States may be summarized as follows:

God is just and merciful. Man's duty is to do justly, love mercy, and walk humbly with his God. When man obeys the will and commandments of God, he receives spiritual rewards; when he disobeys God, he suffers punishment.

All persons are created equal in the sight of God; human equality and the consequent feeling of brotherhood are to be sought by and for all; friendship and hospitality are universal ideals.

All persons possess certain rights because they are part of God's creation; equally important are the responsibilities of all men as children of God.

Dignified labor is a duty of all endowed with the required strength and ability to work. All persons are entitled to the opportunity to participate in constructive dignified labor and in its just rewards.

There should be regular periods of rest after labor, for refreshment of body, mind, and spirit, and for the worship of God.

Man is a steward, or trustee, of the goods of the earth. Only God is the owner. Man is required to account personally for his stewardship.

Individuals should have respect for property rights with the understanding that property rights should be limited by the needs of others in the community.

To pardon or to forgive the transgressions by others against one's person is in accord with God's forgiveness of man; God's forgiveness is conditional upon man's repentance for his errors. Justice should be tempered with mercy.

Individuals should generally plan to marry and to create and shelter families; only in exceptional situations is celibacy required. (The Roman Catholic Church as a rule forbids marriage to those who dedicate their lives to religion.) Family life should be imbued with the spirit of truth, peace, and respect for the human personality.

All men are called upon to witness to their faith by giving thanks for God's love and care and by serving Him. In this sense, laymen, and not clergy alone, are called upon to be a servant people.

The immortality of the person is regarded as one of the distinctive qualities of human life. Man's life on earth is incomplete. The wisdom and love of God are so great that life will be brought to fulfilment after death of the person in this world. Immortality is a gift from a beneficent God.

Birth Control. See p. 88.

Church Buildings. Prosperous times have enabled church organizations to obtain substantial contributions from members to funds for building programs. Annual expenditures by all denominations for new houses of worship and for church school buildings have mounted to a total of about one billion dollars. It is not unusual for suburban groups to construct a church school fully as large and imposing as the church building itself. Often it has been said that the minds of Americans have always run to buildings, but this is not the only or the whole explanation. Local congregations have been constantly increasing in size, and the building boom has been a response to growing constituencies and the desire to carry out programs of activity that are more diversified than in previous times. (See Social Activities, below.)

Church-Related Education. Many of the early institutions of higher education in the United States, the land of colleges, were established by churches in order to provide for the training of clergymen (Harvard, Yale, and Columbia Universities are examples). Although numerous colleges organized for this purpose have long since become independent of church controls, some have remained "church-related," maintaining a variety of relationships ranging from substantial control by a religious body to mere sentimental tribute to the founders. Most of the church-related institutions are liberal arts colleges. There are about 475 Protestant church-related institutions and about 270 Roman Catholic ones; a much smaller number are affiliated with other religious bodies.

Religious organizations have generally assumed full responsibility for educational programs of special interest to them. Protestant bodies maintain numerous theological seminaries and Sunday schools. Roman Catholics also have their theological seminaries, as well as their parochial and diocesan schools for the elementary and high-school grades. Jews have reported an unprecedented increase in attendance at Sabbath and weekly religious schools during the period following the Second World War, and they, too, have established a number of theological seminaries. Many conservative Protestant bodies have organized Bible colleges to train students for their Christian ministries. A few Protestant bodies have their own parochial schools. Recently, in many public school systems interfaith co-operation has made regular instruction available (in the religion chosen by parents and children) in classes that meet during periods of "released time."

Collective Bargaining. See p. 88.

Divorce. See p. 89.

Ecumenism. See p. 85.

Federal Aid for Education. See p. 89.

Four Main Religions. Probably every known emphasis in religion has been manifested among the people of the United States, as reflected in personal and official declarations of belief, functions of religious groups, and the structures of various religious institutions.

Are Americans a religious people? From the statistical data on church membership, some observers obtain evidence of a religious revival, whereas others arrive at a contrary conclusion. Thus, a noted theologian concludes from the figures that Americans are a highly religious people in the sense that a large proportion of the laity participate in the activities of local churches, but he adds that in reality certain non-religious influences and motives determine the decisions of everyday life.

Although the earliest American religious bodies (such as those of the Baptists, Congregationalists, Episcopalians, Friends, Jews, Lutherans, Methodists, Orthodox groups, Presbyterians, Reformed Church organizations, and Roman Catholics) were formed by European immigrants, at least twenty new religious bodies originated in the United States. The latter include the Adventists, Christian Scientists, Christian Churches (Disciples of Christ), Jehovah's Witnesses, Unitarians, and Universalists. Some of the native groups have developed into large denominations.

A long-continued significant trend changed the American nation from a predominantly Protestant people into one in which the Roman Catholic, Jewish, and Eastern Orthodox groups have achieved a prominent role in major cities and in many of the states. By 1890, as reported by the Bureau of the Census, the Roman Catholic Church had more communicants than any other single religious body. Since then the trend in church membership has been upward, rising in most years more rapidly than the general population. At the same time it was reported in 1950 that the two largest religious groups—Protestants and Roman Catholics—had about the same numerical ratio to each other as had been the case half a century earlier.

Since 1950, membership in the Roman Catholic Church has increased at a higher rate than the total membership for the various Protestant denominations. Simultaneously, many Jewish families, moving out of cities to the suburbs, have organized new synagogues and temples, adding to the growing recognition of Judaism as one of the four leading religious groups. The Eastern Churches have also been building new edifices for numerous growing constituencies. Consequently, it may be said that Americans have become in the main a "four-religion" people, despite the fact that there has evolved within the Christian world a sort of "third force" represented by some fifteen religious bodies outside the mainstream of Protestantism. These include the Adventists, the Churches of Christ, Scientist, the Churches of God, the Holiness bodies, the Evangelistic Associations, the Pentecostal Assemblies, and Jehovah's Witnesses.

Healing and Health Activities. Officials representing seventy-two religious bodies in the United States reported healing and health programs in statements submitted to the Bureau of the Census during the most recent survey of religous bodies. The data were as follows: (1) Two religious bodies reported a primary emphasis on healing and health, namely, the Church of Christ, Scientist, and the Divine Science Church. (2) Thirty-five religious bodies reported an emphasis on healing as part of their doctrine, these including the Church of Jesus Christ of Latter-Day Saints, the Reorganized Church of Jesus Christ of Latter-Day Saints, the Churches of God, the Evangelistic Associations, the Pentecostal Assemblies, the Holiness churches, and the Church of the Nazarene. (3) Thirty religious bodies reported the practice of anointing, including the Eastern Orthodox churches, the Old Catholic Church, the Church of the Brethren, and the Roman Catholic Church. (4) Five religious bodies mentioned health practices as part of their general doctrine —including the Seventh Day Adventists and the Salvation Army. In addition to all the foregoing, there are probably quite a few other religious bodies adhering to somewhat similar doctrines on this subject whose officials omitted specific reference to them.

Immigration. See p. 89.

Interfaith Co-operation. The hopes and dreams of many immigrants to the United States for new relationships between men and God and between men themselves—relationships which could not be satisfactorily established in the Old World—have been to some extent realized. There are many free churches in the free society of the New World. At first the free churches functioned in an atmosphere of religious isolationism, but in due time the people and their leaders pursued an aim that would have seemed strange to many of the nation's founders. Church officials and laymen, calling for better understanding and co-operation among religious groups, began to collaborate in various ways, and on some issues they united instead of dividing as hitherto. This trend toward interfaith co-operation was reinforced by the impact of drastic social changes, such as the transition from a rural society with small groups and many interpersonal relationships to a predominantly urban society with large institutions and more impersonal relationships among individuals. The attendant high mobility of the population had a profound effect upon established institutions in city and country.

Backgrounds of Interfaith Co-operation. The earliest programs of co-operation between Protestant denominations were probably those initiated by lay officials of Sunday schools who formed interdenominational associations and by women participants in foreign missions who welcomed the opportunity to work with like-minded people irrespective of membership in a particular denomination. Protestant churches began to organize councils of churches (a few of them going as far back as the first years of the twentieth century), whose activities have expanded greatly during the past few decades. By 1950, there were a number of inter-Protestant national organizations. Twelve of these then merged, together with some Orthodox bodies, into an inclusive national co-operative agency, the National Council of Churches of Christ in the U.S.A. which in 1964 included thirty-one denominations. Today there are other national councils: a National Lutheran Council, a National Holiness Association, a Pentecostal Fellowship of North America, a National Association of Evangelicals, and an American Council of Christian Churches.

The National Catholic War Council, active during the First World War, subsequently continued to function as the National Catholic Welfare Conference. This official agency of the Roman Catholic bishops of the United States is charged with responsibility of promoting unity in Catholic work. Jews and Protestants have co-operated in some programs administered by the Conference.

The three branches of Judaism (Orthodox, Conservative, and Reform) have established the Synagogue Council of America, an agency which provides a variety of services and promotes co-operative programs among their members.

Church Unions. Numerous unions, or mergers, of Protestant religious bodies have been effected in the United States. Among the most significant of these have been the following:

The Methodist Church (1939), a merger of the Methodist Episcopal Church; the Methodist Episcopal Church, South; and the Methodist Protestant Church.

The Evangelical United Brethren Church (1946), a union of the Evangelical Church and the Church of the United Brethren in Christ.

The American Lutheran Church (1961), a merger of three bodies: one of similar name but of German origin; the Evangelical

Lutheran Church (Norwegian); and the United Evangelical Lutheran Church (Danish).

The Unitarian Universalist Association (1961), uniting the Unitarian Churches with the Universalist Church in America.

The United Church of Christ (1961), uniting the Congregational Christian Churches with the Evangelical and Reformed Church, the latter being a union of the Reformed Church in the United States with the Evangelical Synod of North America (1934).

The Lutheran Church in America (1963), a merger of four bodies: the American Evangelical Lutheran Church; the Augustana Evangelical Lutheran Church; the Finnish Evangelical Lutheran Church; and the United Lutheran Church in America.

Recently under discussion has been a proposal, first put forward in 1960 by Eugene Carson Blake, Stated Clerk (chief executive officer) of the Presbyterian Church in the U.S.A., to unite that Church with the Methodist Church, the Protestant Episcopal Church, and the United Church of Christ. In addition, the Disciples of Christ and the Evangelical United Brethren Church have authorized their representatives to participate in the deliberations of these four bodies regarding the proposed merger.

Ecumenism. Increasingly the term *ecumenism* has been used to denote programs of practical co-operation and spiritual unity within and among the principal religious bodies of the world. Important agencies of the Protestant, Eastern Orthodox, Jewish, and Roman Catholic religions have participated in this movement.

The World Council of Churches, founded in 1948 after a long period of preparation, reports a constituency of more than two hundred religious bodies in eighty nations and on all five continents. It is an all-inclusive agency representing Protestant and Eastern Orthodox bodies.

A World Union of Progressive Judaism promotes co-operation among Reform Jewish bodies in many countries; the World Council of Synagogues (Conservative), and the Joint Overseas Commission of the Union of Orthodox Congregations of America carry on similar international programs of mutual understanding and aid.

Pope John XXIII made ecumenism the official business of the Roman Catholic Church by establishing the Secretariat for Promotion of Christian Unity as part of the preparations for the sessions of the Vatican Council (Vatican II) that began in 1962. The broad and free discussions of the Council, which were followed by some forty invited non-Catholic "delegate observers," provided further evidence of the pontiff's intention. Pope John's pioneering in this effort has led to his recognition by Catholics and non-Catholics alike as one of the great figures in the history of organized religion. Similarly, Pope Paul VI declared that he would continue the general policies of his influential predecessor, stating, "We intend to continue the ongoing dialogue." The term *dialogue* now refers to co-operative means of sharing experience, of comparing points of view, and of developing methods to further interfaith understanding.

Jewish-Christian Co-operation. For several decades Jewish and Christian religious groups in many states have worked together to advance their common interests. This type of organized co-operation began with committees of Goodwill appointed by the Federal Council of Churches and the Central Conference of American Rabbis (the Reform Branch of Judaism). Annual joint meetings have been held to explore interfaith problems and co-operative activities.

The National Conference of Christians and Jews (founded in 1928 by Newton D. Baker, Charles Evans Hughes, S. Parkes Cadman, Roger Williams Straus, and Carlton J. H. Hayes) has drawn together large numbers of individuals who have worked in various ways to promote democratic living and mutual respect and goodwill among religious and cultural groups.

An international conference of Christians and Jews was held at Oxford, England, in 1946 on the initiative of the National Conference of Christians and Jews. Four years later, in Paris, the World Brotherhood organization was formed, with offices in New York City as well as abroad. Recently renamed the Council on World Tensions, this organization aims to foster mutual understanding and co-operation among statesmen, educators, and religious leaders in the principal nations of the world.

Mobility. Americans have always been a mobile people. The early movement of large numbers westward from the eastern seaboard colonies was followed by drastic population shifts from farm and village to the city. One family in five moves every year, according to recent sampling studies by the Bureau of the Census. Some move their residence within the same city, many others from one city to another, from city to suburb, or from suburb to suburb. Older people may retire and move to states such as California and Florida for sake of a mild climate. Young people may move in order to keep their jobs or to obtain new ones.

In recent years this high degree of mobility may have brought new members to local congregations, but many of them moved again before the relationship became well established. Consequently, high mobility tended to make life impersonal, especially in city and suburbs as contrasted with small rural communities.

Frequent changes in residence encouraged church members in many denominations to change their religious affiliations so that it was not uncommon for local congregations to have a substantial proportion of members who had previously belonged to twenty or thirty bodies. Laymen thus became increasingly aware of the common elements among the denominations, at least in many Protestant bodies, and lost interest in the differences between them. Thus, high mobility, in addition to making life more impersonal, resulted in a partial amalgamation of religious beliefs and programs.

Relief and Reconstruction. Since 1945 about 600,000 refugees have been admitted as immigrants to the United States under the provisions of special legislation. Most of them have been resettled with the practical assistance of Jewish, Eastern Orthodox, Roman Catholic, and Protestant agencies. The various organizations have provided sponsorship, technical advice, transportation, loans, and the fellowship of local parishes and congregations. The principal religious organizations have also continued their extensive programs of relief and reconstruction among the needly abroad which they had initiated prior to the Second World War. Church-related relief agencies have functioned effectively by collecting funds and distributing medicines, clothing, bedding, and food. In addition, religious agencies have received large quantities of food from the surpluses stored by the United States government for free distribution abroad.

World-wide services of this kind have been entirely consistent with the record of innumerable social welfare functions that religious agencies have performed from the earliest times. Today, as in the past, the religious bodies administer or sponsor hospitals, homes for the aged, child care institutions, community centers, and the like. Methods of control vary with the denomination. Roman Catholic social welfare organizations are controlled by the parishes and dioceses. Jewish agencies, once closely related to the local congregations, are now organizations representing the entire community, encouraged and supported by the congregations. Protestant hospitals and social welfare agencies are variously related to the religious bodies, some with direct control and administration, others with either contractual or informal connections.

Intermarriage. See p. 89.

Prayer in Public Schools. See p. 89.

Public Issues. Resolutions passed by American religious bodies on public issues are both frequent and controversial. The representatives of Christian churches and those of Jewish congregations are accustomed to speaking out at regular meetings and on other occasions. There are well-known disagreements on these matters, as well as common elements, interests, and even parallels. The following comments summarize briefly certain positions taken by religious bodies on selected public issues. The sources are official documents issued by these bodies. It should be borne in mind, however, that not all bodies have declared themselves on all the issues listed, and that in many instances the official positions may or may not be fully accepted by significant sections of the constituencies.

(1) *Birth Control.* Various methods of birth control are widely approved in Judaism and Protestantism. Birth control is opposed by Eastern Churches; if effected by artificial means, it is opposed by the Roman Catholic Church, which has approved family limitation by the rhythm method.

(2) *Collective Bargaining.* The right of employers as well as that of employees to organize, with mutual obligations to promote the public interest, has been generally affirmed by religious bodies which have expressed themselves on this issue. (The earliest statement was that of Pope Leo XIII in 1891.) Religious bodies have often advocated minimum wage laws and have stressed the need for public action to provide social security.

(3) *Community Co-operation.* Certain public issues related to problems of health, poverty, slums, and the like have aroused religious groups to participate in remedial programs of the community. Co-operation with community agencies such as Community Chests and United Funds is widely advocated, as are the joint study and systematized discussion of the social problems by means of "dialogue."

(4) *Divorce.* Protestant religious groups generally disapprove or discourage the practice of divorce, though remarriage in the church is usually permitted under certain conditions. Many Protestant bodies have issued no official statement on this subject. Jewish groups sanction divorce after true marriage has ceased. Roman Catholics do not consent to any final divorce of persons who may marry again, but separations may be approved, and decrees of nullity can be granted by the diocesan courts and Vatican Rota (tribunal of appeal) in exceptional cases.

(5) *Federal Aid for Education.* This issue has proved to be extremely divisive. Most Roman Catholics favor general federal aid to private as well as public elementary and secondary schools, whereas Protestant, Jews, and members of the Eastern Churches usually oppose the use of public funds for private schools. Consequently, aid for specific projects in higher education seems to meet with more general approval than aid for elementary and secondary education, and this specific type as well as certain forms of specialized assistance have been made available frequently. A minority in religious circles oppose all forms of federal aid to education.

(6) *Immigration.* The principal religious bodies have taken a stand in favor of more liberal provisions for the admission of orphans, refugees, and other immigrants than are allowed for under present law; some advocate abolition of the quotas based on national origin, while others would at least make the quota system more flexible.

(7) *Intermarriage.* This practice is widely disapproved by many religious bodies, especially by the conservative Protestants, the Eastern Churches, the Orthodox Jews, and the Roman Catholics. The last-named have special regulations for intermarriage when approved by the bishop of a diocese, the couple pledging to have their offspring baptized and brought up in the Roman Catholic faith.

(8) *Prayer in Public Schools.* This practice has been one of the more divisive influences; it is generally favored by many Roman Catholics and the more conservative Protestants but opposed by many liberal Protestants and by Jews.

(9) *Race Relations.* Religious bodies generally favor interracial co-operation, including programs to eradicate prejudice; integrated churches, schools, and colleges; and recognition of the unique

values in every person of whatever race. On the centenary of President Lincoln's Emancipation Proclamation, four hundred representatives of religious bodies assembled in response to an invitation by the Synagogue Council of America, the National Catholic Welfare Conference, and the National Council of Churches. An "appeal to the conscience of the American people" was issued, and a program to improve housing conditions for Negroes in ten cities was started. Prominent officials of some religious bodies also identified themselves with Negro groups sponsoring demonstrations in behalf of their civil rights. The active support of many religious groups was a major factor in enacting the 1964 Federal Civil Rights law.

(10) *Social Action.* A variety of public issues arise from time to time, resulting in demands upon the churches for remedial programs of social action. It has always been easier to assert social ideals for all mankind than it has been to implement them in the home town. It is easier to approve the aims and methods of the United Nations than it is to decide what kind of housing program should be promoted in a given community.

(11) *United Nations.* American religious bodies (apparently almost universally) approve the aims and general methods of the United Nations. They have given wide support specifically to joint projects such as technical assistance to underdeveloped nations, the Freedom from Hunger Campaign of the Food and Agricultural Organization, and the like.

Revivals. In 1821 the attorney Charles G. Finney reported that he had received a mighty baptism of the Holy Ghost while on his knees in his law office, and he called for a revival meeting, the first of four well-organized national mass revivals which have occurred in the United States at intervals of about forty-five years. The leaders were, successively, Finney, Dwight L. Moody (1837–1899), Billy Sunday (1862–1935), and Billy Graham (1918–), Historians, clergymen, and laymen have advanced various explanations for these mass phenomena. They seem to have occurred when one or more of the following conditions were present: a widespread feeling of a special need for religion in national and personal life; dissatisfaction among many sincerely devoted people with the state of the world and the state of the religious bodies; broad theological discussion; and the rise of a strong personality associated with these developments.

(Officials of religious bodies have differed widely in their estimates of the results of these mass revivals. There have been many revivals in addition to those mentioned above; some led to the formation of religious organizations such as the Pentecostal Assemblies and the Churches of God.)

Race Relations. See p. 89.

Separation of Church and State. Among the Founding Fathers, it was Thomas Jefferson who stressed most emphatically the need for a "wall of separation" between church and state. While some later political and religious leaders regarded this proposal as naive or impossible—since the church and the state were bound to interact in various ways—the "separation of church and state" is now widely accepted by the religious groups of the nation as a desirable goal. In 1948, for example, the Roman Catholic bishops of the United States declared in a formal statement that they favored a policy of no "special privilege to any group and no restriction on the religious liberty of any citizens." Jews, Protestants, and members of the Eastern Orthodox churches have made similar statements.

Social Activities in Local Churches. "We marvel at how you Americans eat in your churches," a European visitor remarked after visiting many churches in the United States. It is not unusual for churches to include large, well-equipped kitchens, from which meals can be served on special occasion.

The "seven-day church" has become a meaningful term, reflecting not only the full use of buildings as centers of social activities but also the very active role of laymen in the congregations of most faiths. Observers from abroad are astonished at the initiative of laymen in handling church finances, at the independence displayed by women's organizations in many local churches, at the lively discussion of current issues by young people, and at the spirit of informal fellowship developed among clergy and communicants.

Translations of Scriptures. Significant new translations of the Scriptures have recently been made available by Jewish, Catholic, and Protestant denominations. Among the English versions most widely used in the United States today are the following:

For Jews, the Hebrew Scriptures in one translation was sponsored by the Jewish Publication Society in 1917; subsequently another translation was planned by the same society (of which the Torah was published in 1962, with other books in preparation).

For Roman Catholics, the Rheims-Douai texts were revised by Bishop Richard Challoner of London (1749–1750); recent editions were sponsored by the Confraternity of Christian Doctrine (beginning with the New Testament in 1941, continued later with portions of the Old Testament, and with further translation now proceeding).

For Protestants, the Authorized Version (the "King James Bible") of 1611 is still the most widely used Bible, called the "noblest monument of English prose." The Revised Standard Version (New Testament in 1946 and the entire Bible in 1952), a translation sponsored by the National Council of Churches, has been extensively distributed. The New English Bible (New Testament published in 1961), a translation by scholars from several Protestant denominations, has also been favorably received in the United States.

A significant recent event was the publication in Scotland of a Roman Catholic edition of the New Testament in the Revised Standard Version. This edition, embodying only a few changes, is for private reading, not for use in the Mass. (The initiative was solely that of the British Catholics; the Protestant translators of the Revised Standard Version gave their approval.) The edition is to be made available in the United States.

United Nations. See p. 90.

PART THREE

GLOSSARY OF RELIGIOUS TERMS

The following definitions of frequently used terms will be helpful in study or discussion of religions in the United States. In some cases, several definitions are given in order to reflect the views of the principal religious groups.

Absolution: A rite (administered by a clergyman after confession and the promise of penance) which releases the individual from the consequences of his guilt and from punishment for his sin.

Adventist: A believer in (or a member of a religious body that believes in) the imminent second coming of Christ to earth.

Allah: In Islam, the name of the Supreme Being or all-powerful God.

Allegory: An extended description of one thing to symbolize or take the form of another.

Anointing: The application of oil in a ceremonial for the purpose of healing or consecration.

Apocalyptic: Pertaining to (or in the nature of) a revelation.

Apocrypha: A group of books excluded by Protestants from the Bible as not sufficiently authoritative, though worthy of study for their religious and historical value; sometimes printed between the Old and New Testaments; separately printed in some versions of the Bible.

Apostle: Originally one of the twelve disciples chosen by Jesus to preach, teach, and heal. Matthias was chosen to take the place of Judas after the Crucifixion. Later, Paul and other early leaders were considered to be Apostles.

Apostolic: Pertaining to a teaching or practice of the Apostles, or to an Apostle named by Christ or to early Christian Church.

Apostolic succession: A theory of continuing succession in the episcopacy and leadership of the churches, maintained from apostolic times to the present; strictly emphasized in the Eastern,

Roman Catholic, Anglican, and certain Protestant communions.

Arminian: Pertaining to the system of thought (or to the followers) of Arminius, a Dutch Protestant theologian (1560–1609), who denied certain of John Calvin's teachings and taught a more lenient doctrine of God's grace and man's salvation as offered not only to the "elect" but to all believers.

Atonement: In Christian theology, Christ's redemption of man and reconciliation of man to God.

Autocephalous: The condition of being independent in jurisdiction, as in the several branches of the Eastern Orthodox churches.

Baptism: Application of water to a person by immersion, sprinkling or pouring (affusion), in a ceremonial as a sign of removal of sin and of admission into a Christian church; in a few Christian churches, baptism is of the Holy Spirit, without application of water.

Bible: In Judaism, the Holy Scriptures, a collection of 28 books, corresponding to the Old Testament of Christian bodies; in Protestantism, a collection of 66 books, 39 in the Old Testament and 27 in the New Testament; in Roman Catholicism, a collection of 73 books, 46 in the Old Testament (including books placed in the Apocrypha by Protestants), and 27 in the New Testament.

Calvinist: A follower of John Calvin (1509–1564); pertaining to Calvin's teachings (which emphasized an elect to be saved), doctrines that have since been considerably redefined and interpreted by Calvinist churches.

Canon: The books admitted to the Bible by standards of authority and authenticity, hence considered by religious bodies to contain the word of God and to be the source of faith and the rule of life.

Christ: The Messiah or "Anointed One" expected by the Jews as the ideal ruler; in Christian theology, Jesus is believed to be the fulfilment of this prophecy, as well as the Son of God and the Son of Man; the second person in the Trinity, the Saviour and Redeemer of mankind.

Christian: A follower of Christ; the term was first used in Antioch as recorded in Acts; it is derived from the Greek work for "Anointed," *Christos*.

Church: The community of Christian believers; it is locally organized in individual churches, first recorded in Acts as groups that met for prayer, teaching, fellowship, and breaking bread in commemoration of Christ.

Classis: In the Reformed churches a district association consisting of ministers and elders, which supervises the local churches; also the church district governed by the classis; the term corresponds to the presbytery in the Presbyterian churches.

Communion: *See* Lord's Supper.

Confession: An admission of sin to a clergyman or upon conversion; the distinctive formulation of the beliefs of a religious body; a term sometimes used to designate a large group or family or religious bodies.

Confirmation: The ceremony by which a person is admitted to full membership in a church; also ratification of the action of a church organization by a higher authority.

Congregationalist: Pertaining to a form of church government in which there is no superior authority over the local congregation.

Conversion: The act of accepting a religion or of changing from one religion to another; this act may be instantaneous or gradual.

Covenant: An expression of God's love and grace toward man. In the Old Testament it is regarded as a sacred bond between God and man and between man and man, especially God's promise to Israel, first given through Abraham; in the New Testament it expresses God's relation to man in terms of communion in Christ and the indwelling of the Holy Spirit.

Creed: A formulation of the principal beliefs of a religious body.

Decalogue (Ten Commandments): A summary of God's requirements of man as handed down to Moses and recorded in the Old Testament.

Dharma: In Buddhism and Hinduism, a term for the reality upon which the law of truth and virtue is based; the law of truth and virtue itself.

Disciples: In the New Testament, the followers of Jesus; later, sometimes synonymous with the apostles.

Doctrine: A teaching or a position of a religious body or of a theologian.

Dogma: A principle, or a system of principles, setting forth the teachings of a religious body.

Ecumenical: World-wide, generally referring to movements for unity among religious bodies.

Episcopal: Pertaining to a system of church government in which bishops have supervisory authority and other functions; pertaining to bishops and the episcopacy.

Epistle: One of the books of the New Testament, in the form of letters containing broad commentaries on the life and teachings of Christ.

Eschatology: Doctrine concerning "the last things," or the ultimate condition of man, the world, and history in relation to God.

Esoteric: Intended for and understood only by an inner group (often applied to the language used to reveal a message to this group and conceal it from outsiders).

Eucharist: *See* Lord's Supper.

Evangelical: Indicating direct loyalty to the gospel of Christ; reference to a group of churches claiming this emphasis (in contrast to the ecclesiastical system or to rationalist thinking on religion); zeal for the Christian life as distinguished from mere ritual.

Excommunication: The action whereby a church excludes from communion with the faithful a person found guilty of speech, practice, or belief forbidden by that church. Such a person is still subject to the ordinary obligations, and he may by penance and amendment of conduct be restored to full membership.

Fall of man: In Christian teaching, man's estrangement from God through sin, as symbolized by Adam's and Eve's disobedience.

Fundamentalist: A person holding to the infallibility of the Bible text and related teachings, believing that they must be accepted literally.

Glossolalia: *See* Speaking in tongues.

God: The object of true worship; in Scripture and religious literature, referred to as One, Creator, Almighty, Most High, Holy One, Father, and Redeemer; revealed in nature by such terms as Grace, Mercy, Justice, Love; revealed in the New Testament through the life, teachings, death, and resurrection of Jesus Christ, and in the work of the Holy Spirit; the first person of the Trinity.

Gospel ("Good News"): The broad New Testament name for the message of Jesus Christ; one of the first four books of the New

Testament. (Of the four Gospels, Matthew, Mark, and Luke sum up the life of Christ in much the same sequence and are called Synoptic Gospels; John is more philosophical.)

Grace: God's freely given redemptive love for man; in the New Testament, grace is regarded as made manifest in Jesus Christ.

Healing, gift of: Spiritual powers over disease and infirmity, recorded as given by God to prophets, Jesus, and the Apostles; later attributed to persons with special insights and talents.

Hierarchy: A system of government by the clergy; the arrangement of those governing the church in the order of their authority.

Holiness: A state of spiritual purity; the quality of persons designated for religious service.

Holy Spirit (Holy Ghost): The third person of the Trinity in Christian theology. (In the Old Testament the term is applied to many of the acts of God, His creation, inspiration of prophets, rulers, and others, and to God's convenant with Israel. In the New Testament, the term is applied to the inner, personal workings of God both within the Church and within the human heart.)

Immaculate Conception, doctrine of: The teaching that the Virgin Mary was conceived free from original sin.

Immanent: Indwelling; referring to the presence of God's power and spirit within man and the world.

Incarnation: In Christian theology, God's becoming man in Jesus Christ.

Infallibility, doctrine of: A teaching that the Scriptures are free from error; in the Roman Catholic Church, the term "papal infallibility" is applied to the teaching of the Pope when he speaks as head of the Church on matters of faith and morals.

Israel: The name (meaning "contender with God") given to Jacob after his wrestling with an angel; the name of Jacob's descendants: the Hebrews, the Jews, and their nation. (When the Kingdom was divided in antiquity, the Northern Kingdom was named Israel, and the Southern, Judah. A new republic, Israel, was established in Palestine in 1948.)

Jehovah: The Hebrew name for God, used in the Holy Scriptures of the Jews, the Old Testament of the Christians.

Jesus Christ: *See* Christ.

Judaism: The religion of the Jewish people, recorded and interpreted in the Holy Scriptures of the Jews, i.e., the Old Testament of the Christians, and the Talmud.

Justification: The state of right relationship with God; in Christian theology, being saved through faith in Jesus Christ as Lord and Saviour.

Karma: In Buddhism and Hinduism, an act of piety; the doctrine that forces accumulated within the individual determine his personality and experience; the principle of causalty (applied, for example, to the moral causal sequence).

Kingdom of God: God's reign, prophesied by the apocalyptic writers in the Old Testament; in the New Testament, it refers to the spiritual kingdom, both as manifest in Jesus Christ and as still to come in the final triumph of God.

Law: Divine commandments and rules formulated by Moses and his successors, as recorded in the Bible, particularly in the first five books of the Bible (the Pentateuch); the Pentateuch; the Torah.

Liturgy: A form of public worship, as required or preferred. (Certain religious bodies that carry on uniform or mainly uniform worship, in contrast to informal, optional services, are called *liturgical*.)

Logos: In Christian theology, Christ as the Word, eternally generated from the substance of God the Father; the second person of the Trinity.

Lord's Supper: The sacrament of the Eucharist, or Holy Communion, being the partaking of bread and wine as emblems of the flesh and blood of Christ, in commemoration of Him, as at the last supper with His disciples; variously interpreted in the theologies of different churches.

Mass: The principal service of worship in the Roman Catholic Church and in the parishes of the High Church party of the Anglican communion.

Messiah: Hebrew word, meaning "the Anointed One." (In the Bible the Messiah is the ideal deliverer or ruler expected by the Jews; in Christian theology, the prophecy is regarded as fulfilled through Jesus Christ, Son of Man and Son of God, Saviour of the World.) (*See* Christ.)

Miracle: In Biblical terms a work of God, regarded as either independent of or contrary to the known course or laws of the natural world.

Modernist: In contrast to Fundamentalist, one who interprets the Scriptures in the light of modern scholarship and the findings of science.

Mysticism: The belief that direct knowledge or insight of God or of truth can be obtained through spiritual power, independent of or transcending reason.

Ordinance: A ceremonial prescribed by a religious body.

Papal infallibility: *See* Infallibility.

Parable: A short narrative describing a possible occurrence, told for the purpose of conveying moral or spiritual teaching.

Passover: A yearly festival of the Jews, celebrating their having been spared from God's smiting of the first-born in Egypt and their subsequent escape from Egyptian slavery.

Pentecost: A yearly Jewish harvest festival. It is celebrated by Christians as the day of the Holy Spirit's descent on the disciples of Christ, as recorded in Acts.

Pentecostal: Pertaining to the descent of the Holy Ghost upon the disciples of Christ at the time of a Jewish Pentecost, as recorded in Acts; pertaining to an experience upon conversion to Christ; the name of a group of Protestant religious bodies.

Presbytery: An association of representatives of local churches under the presbyterian form of church government, which supervises the local churches; the district governed by a presbytery.

Priest: The ordained clergyman in certain religious bodies who is authorized to conduct worship and to perform the other designated duties of the office.

Prophets: In the Old Testament, unique semipublic leaders, speakers for God. (They proclaimed the religious ideals of the people, expressed ethical concerns and convictions, and interpreted historical events in terms of God's purpose, often criticizing the social order and advocating justice and reform on behalf of its victims.)

Publican: A tax collector in ancient Rome and its provinces.

Purgatory: In Roman Catholic teaching, a condition after death in which those who die in God's grace are cleansed of venial sins, and satisfy divine justice for mortal sins, by undergoing varying degrees of punishment before being admitted to heaven.

Redemption: In theology, God's deliverance of man; in the New Testament specifically, deliverance from sin and death into a new life through the atonement of Jesus Christ.

Resurrection: Rising from the dead; in Christian theology, the rising of Christ from the dead, evidenced by His empty tomb and His appearance to the disciples after the Crucifixion, and hence the rising from the dead of those who believe in Him.

Revelation: Communication of spiritual truth by removal of all barriers, especially by divine action.

Ritual: The form prescribed or recommended for conducting a religious ceremony.

Sabbatarian: One who in belief and practice observes the seventh day (Saturday) as the Sabbath.

Sacrament: A religious ceremony observed by Christians, believed to have been initiated by Christ, the number varying in different religious bodies. A sacrament is a rite possessing two parts: a physical sign and a spiritual good or result.

Saint: In the New Testament, a term sometimes applied to faithful members of the early Church; in later usage, an exceptionally holy person canonized by a religious body, or one regarded as exceptionally holy by friends and associates.

Salvation: A state of spiritual health; the rescue of a person from sin and other evils by God's power so that he may attain blessedness. (In Christian teaching, salvation is accomplished through Jesus Christ.)

Sanctification: The operation of the Holy Spirit within a person, enabling him to be led to holiness.

Second Coming: The return of Jesus Christ to the earth, an event expected by Adventist denominations and by many individuals in other religious bodies.

See: The place from which a bishop exercises his jurisdiction; the jurisdiction of a bishop.

Speaking in tongues: Utterances accompanying conversion or holiness, either in languages not the person's own or in ecstatic speech incomprehensible to others and sometimes to the speaker himself. (The precedent is the effect of the Holy Spirit on the disciples of Christ at Pentecost, as recorded in Acts.)

Synagogue: The local organization and place for worship of a Jewish congregation.

Synod: A church council or assembly, meeting at intervals to exercise the functions entrusted to it under a particular system of church government.

Synoptic Gospels: *See* Gospel.

Ten Commandments: *See* Decalogue.

Testament: A term that means "covenant" (not "will") in Biblical usage.

Torah: *See* Law.

Transcendent: A term applied to God, meaning that He is prior to, above, and supreme in relation to the universe that He created and rules.

Trinity: In Christian theology, the union in one divine nature of God the Father, God the Son, and God the Holy Spirit, regarded as a revelation that cannot be adequately explained in words.

Unction: An anointing in a ceremonial, as of a person believed to be in danger of death.

Unitarian: Pertaining to the teaching of the strict humanity of Jesus, thus denying the trinitarian concept of God.

Part Four

SUMMARY OF STATISTICS

The statistics in this section were derived mainly from official reports of religious bodies published in directories and annuals or in the *Yearbook of American Churches* (a reference work compiling information from all faiths). Note that the summary begins with general information, followed by statistics for religious groups described in Part One and, lastly, by useful information about religious schools, foreign missions, church attendance, and estimated membership figures for the world's principal denominations.

General Information. Perhaps 90 per cent of the parishes or congregations of all faiths own their houses of worship, the remainder meeting in homes, rented halls, and churches belonging to other local religious groups. Although there have been no over-all surveys of this factor since 1936, it is known that many newly organized congregations start operating without a building of their own; therefore, the 90 per cent figure based on Federal Censuses of Religious Bodies in 1906, 1916, 1926, and 1936 may still be approximately correct today.

Statistics for aggregate church membership and information about the number of local churches are published (annually or at other regular intervals) by all but a few of the 250 bodies that were included in the 1936 Census of Religious Bodies. These now report to the *Yearbook of American Churches,* from which (1964 edition) the following information for 1962 is mainly derived:

NUMBER OF CHURCHES AND OF MEMBERS, BY RELIGIOUS GROUPS

Religious Group	No. of Bodies Reporting Membership	No. of Churches	No. of Members
Buddhist	1	55	60,000
Old Catholic, Polish National Catholic, and Armenian Church of North America, Dioceses	7	348	597,372
Eastern Churches	20	1,454	3,001,751
Jewish Congregations *	1	4,079	5,509,000
Roman Catholic	1	23,412	43,847,938
Protestant	222	289,892	64,929,941
Totals	252	319,240	117,946,002

* Includes Orthodox, Conservative, and Reform.

The same source gives the following figures for the clergy:

CLERGY, BY RELIGIOUS GROUPS

Religious Group	No. of Bodies Reporting Pastors with Charges	No. of Pastors with Charges	Total Number of Clergy
Buddhist	1	75	90
Old Catholic, Polish National Catholic, and Armenian Church of North America, Diocese	7	321	422
Eastern Churches	19	1,309	1,857
Jewish Congregations *	1	3,790	5,120
Roman Catholic	1	17,298	56,818
Protestant	202	223,807	300,168
Totals	231	246,600	364,475

* Includes Orthodox, Conservative, and Reform.

The above tables are at this writing the latest national compilation. However, the various bodies issue reports at irregular intervals, and some have published more recent figures.

Since the most comprehensive Federal Census of Religious Bodies was that for 1926, that year is often used as a basis for comparison with later information or estimates. No important change seems to have occurred in the procedure for reporting membership figures. Roman Catholics, the Eastern Orthodox group, Jewish congregations, the Old Catholics, the Episcopalians, and the Lutherans report on an inclusive, or population, basis; most Protestant bodies report only those persons who have attained full membership (for which the minimum age is usually thirteen).

Since 1926 the average size of congregations of all faiths has increased from 235 to 370, a gain of 59 per cent.

Protestants reported membership totals of 31,511,701 in 1926 and 64,929,941 in 1962. Thus they comprised about 27.0 per cent of the population in 1926, about 34.9 per cent of the population in 1962.

Roman Catholics reported membership totals of 18,605,003 in 1926 and 43,847,938 in 1962. They comprised about 16.0 per cent of the population in 1926, about 23.6 per cent in 1962.

The Church of Christ, Scientist, does not furnish figures of affiliation. The Federal Census of Religious Bodies, 1936, reported a membership of 268,915 in that group.

Statistics for Religious Bodies in Part One. The religious described in Part One are listed below, with recent membership figures. Most of the groups with fewer than 100,000 members (as reported to the *Yearbook of American Churches, 1964*) are omitted, but figures are given for certain well-known families of denominations.

Adventists (5 bodies): 372,972 members. (Of these, one body, the Seventh Day Adventists, reports 335,765.)

Bahá'í: 5,000 members (as reported in Mead's *Handbook of Denominations,* 1961).

Baptists (28 bodies): 21,643,490 members. Of these, the Southern Baptist Convention reported 10,191,303: National Baptist Convention, U.S.A., Inc., 5,000,000; National Baptist Convention of America, 2,668,799; and American Baptist Convention, 1,544,-505.

Brethren, German Baptist (41 bodies): 250,227 members. Of these, the Church of the Brethren reported 201,220; Plymouth Brethren, 33,250; and River Brethren (3 bodies), 8,698.

Buddhists: 60,000 members in the mainland United States, in addition to a larger membership of approximately 160,000 in Hawaii.

Christian and Missionary Alliance: 61,761 members.

Christian Churches (Disciples of Christ) and Churches of Christ: 4,029,046 members.

Christian Science (i.e., Church of Christ, Scientist): No current figures published; 268,915 members (the Census of Religious Bodies, 1936).

Churches of God (12 bodies): 999,542 members. Of these, Assemblies of God report 514,532; Church of God, Cleveland, Tennessee, 179,651; and Church of God, Anderson, Indiana, 145,-241.

Congregationalists: see United Church of Christ.

Eastern Churches (20 bodies): 3,001,751. Of these the Greek Archdiocese of North and South America reports 1,500,000.

Ethical Culture (i.e., American Ethical Union): 7,050 members.

Evangelistic Associations (9 bodies): 66,716 members. Of these, the Christian Congregation reports 39,140.

Federated Churches: 88,411 members (Census of Religious Bodies, 1936).

Friends (8 bodies): 128,495 members. Of these, the Five Years Meeting reports 71,552.

Fundamentalists (i.e., Independent Fundamentalist Churches): 90,040 members.

Holiness bodies: Figures reported under Pentecostal Assemblies, Churches of God, and other groups (see descriptions in Part One).

Independent churches: 40,276 (Census of Religious Bodies, 1936).

Indians' religious groups: No estimates for native religions are available; Protestants and Roman Catholics are included in the reports of those bodies.

Informal fellowships: No constituencies are reported, because their members also belong to various other religious bodies.

International Church of the Foursquare Gospel: 89,562 members.

Jehovah's Witnesses: 286,908 members.

Jewish Congregations: 5,509,000 members.

Latter-Day Saints (5 bodies): 1,846,841 members. Of these, the Church of Jesus Christ of Latter Day Saints reports 1,682,096; and the Reorganized Church of Jesus Christ of Latter Day Saints, 159,336.

Lutherans (11 bodies): 8,356,856 members. Of these, the Lutheran Church in America reports 3,080,272; Lutheran Church—Missouri Synod, 2,522,095; and The American Lutheran Church, 2,338,959.

Mennonites (12 bodies): 164,440 members. Of these, the Mennonite Church reports 75,949.

Methodists (21 bodies): 12,739,925 members. Of these, the Methodist Church reports 10,153,003; the African Methodist Episcopal Church, 1,166,301; The African Methodist Episcopal Zion Church, 770,000; and the Christian Methodist Episcopal Church, 444,493.

Moravians (2 bodies): 67,807 members. Of these, the Moravian Church in America reports 61,777.

Muslims: The small centers of worship submit no reports of members.

Nazarenes (i.e., Church of the Nazarene): 323,491 members.

New Jerusalem, Churches of (Swedenborgian) (2 bodies): 5,854 members.

Old Catholics (5 bodies): 159,961 members.

Pentecostal Assemblies (12 bodies): 404,611 members. Of these, the United Pentecostal Church reports 150,000; and the Pentecostal Church of God in America, 112,000.

Polish National Catholic Church: 282,411 members.

Presbyterians (10 bodies): 4,361,344 members. Of these, the United Presbyterian Church in the U.S.A. reports 3,265,234 members; the Presbyterian Church in the U.S., 928,055; and the Cumberland Presbyterian Church, 82,190.

Protestant Episcopal Church: 3,317,870 members.

Protestantism: Statistics reported in "General Information" above and in separate reports herein.

Reformed Churches (6 bodies): 507,751 members. Of these, the Christian Reformed Church reports 256,015; and the Reformed Church in America, 231,771.

Roman Catholics: 43,847,938 members.

Salvation Army: 259,995 members.

Small Sects: No separate reports of membership are available.

Unitarians and Universalists: 153,689 members.

United Church of Christ: 2,056,696 members.

Vedanta: 5,000 members (Mead's *Handbook of Denominations,* 1961).

Yoga: No reports are available.
Zen: No reports are available.

Protestant Sunday and Sabbath Schools. The religious bodies have always assumed responsibility for education. The Sunday (or Sabbath) school is the type emphasized by Protestants and Jews. The parish (or parochial) school is the principal type among Roman Catholics and a small proportion of Protestants.

Protestant Sunday Schools originated in England, the one started by Robert Raikes at Gloucester in 1780 often being cited as the "first." The total enrollments in Sunday or Sabbath Schools in the United States, as reported by denominational officials to the *Yearbook of American Churches,* are as follows:

Year	*Total Enrollment*
1952	30,680,661
1962	40,096,624

Jewish Education. The synagogue has always been a center for teaching as well as worship. The enrollments in all types of Jewish schools (combining congregational and noncongregational, elementary and secondary, full-time and part-time) reported in the *American Jewish Yearbook* for 1953 and 1963, were as follows:

Year	*Total Enrollment*
1952	336,084
1962	588,955

Of the total 1962 enrollment of 588,955 pupils, 212,804 were enrolled in schools of Reform Judaism, 201,912 in Conservative schools, and 124,395 in Orthodox schools, with the remainder in noncongregational, intercongregational, and other schools whose denominational affiliation was not reported.

Statistics for Roman Catholic Elementary and Secondary Schools. The enrollments in elementary and secondary schools reported in the *Official Catholic Directory,* were as follows:

Year	*Parochial Elementary Schools*	*Diocesan Secondary Schools*
1952	2,838,071	361,852
1962	4,312,082	546,259

NOTE: In addition, there also were 216,000 pupils in "private" Catholic secondary schools in 1952, and 340,036 in 1962.

Roman Catholic parishes also offer religious instruction to public school pupils, the totals given in the *Official Catholic Directory* being:

Year	*Public School Children Receiving Religious Instruction*
1952	2,104,624
1962	3,418,176

Attendance at Worship. Reports based on a sample of civilian adults in the United States who were asked whether they had attended a church service during the week preceding the interview have been published at various times. Those made by the American Institute of Public Opinion (Princeton, New Jersey) which are syndicated in many newspapers, are as follows:

Year	*Per Cent of Adults Attending Church*
1939	41
1940	37
1942	36
1947	45
1950	39
1954	46
1955	49
1956	46
1957	47
1958	49
1959	47
1960	47
1961	47
1962	46
1963	46

Research studies of the figures for selected years indicate that women attend somewhat more frequently than men, and that Roman Catholics attend most regularly. The religious bodies themselves do not report attendance.

Women in the Ministry. Some eighty Protestant bodies in the United States ordain or license women to carry on the ministry. The number of women ordained to the ministry is comparatively small, however, possibly not exceeding 4 per cent of all ordained ministers. Moreover, only a small proportion of ordained women have charge of parishes or congregations. They tend to be employed only as assistant pastors, directors of religious education, teachers, foreign missionaries, and the like. As a rule, parishes will not consider the employment of women as senior ministers in charge.

Some of the well-known religious bodies that ordain women are: The Methodist Church, the United Presbyterian Church in the U.S.A., the United Church of Christ, the Christian Churches (Disciples of Christ), the Baptist Churches, and the Unitarian Universalist Churches.

The number of women in the ministry is not reported regularly; approximate figures based upon denominational statistics appeared in the *Information Service* of the National Council of Churches (May 31, 1952, and March 6, 1954). The latest count disclosed 5,791 ordained women in denominations that publish such reports. The Population Census of 1950 reported 6,777 women clergymen.

Religion Reported by American Civilians. The question, "What is your religion?" was asked in 1957 of a sampling of persons over 14 years of age in 35,000 households containing a total of some 100,000 persons. That survey was conducted by the Federal Bureau of the Census. The replies received were then "extrapolated" to the entire civilian population over age 14, resulting in an estimated total of 139,330,000 as of March, 1957. "Related children under 14 years old by religion reported for the family head and his wife" were also enumerated. A summary of the survey findings follows:

RELIGIONS REPORTED BY AMERICAN CIVILIANS

Religion	Persons 14 Years Old and Over	Per Cent Distribution	Related Children under 14, with Family Head and Wife Reported in Same Religious Group	Per Cent Distribution
Total	119,333,000	100.0	44,397,000	100.0
Protestant	78,952,000	66.2	30,558,000	68.8
Roman Catholic	30,669,000	25.7	11,757,000	26.5
Jewish	3,868,000	3.2	1,107,000	2.5
Other religions	1,545,000	1.3	388,000	0.9
No religion	3,195,000	2.7	502,000	1.1
Religion not reported	1,104,000	0.9	85,000	0.2

Only the data for members of the four largest Protestant families or groups of denominations were tabulated separately. The total of 78,952,000 persons included:

Baptist	23,525,000
Lutheran	8,417,000
Presbyterian	6,656,000
Other Protestant	26,676,000

NOTE: See *Current Population Reports, Series No. 79* (Washington, D.C., 25: Bureau of the Census, 1958), p. 20. The question was not repeated in the Population Census of 1960.

Foreign Missions. From comparatively modest beginnings, Protestant and Roman Catholic churches have developed an expanding foreign mission enterprise. There were 26,390 Protestant missionaries in 1960, sent out by 312 agencies of Protestant churches. This figure represented an increase of 80 per cent since 1950. These missionaries worked in most of the countries in the world (there were none in Afghanistan or in the Communist People's Republic of China, and very few in the Communist countries of eastern Europe and in some Arab areas). Workers had been sent out to India and Japan by 108 foreign mission agencies; Hong Kong and the Philippines had missionary workers from 58 societies in the United States. The income of all foreign mission agencies totaled nearly $164,000,000 in 1960, equivalent to an average annual contribution of $2.75 per Protestant church member. The missionaries sent out from the United States, numbering 26,390, constituted more than 60 per cent of the total number (42,250) of Protestant missionaries sent out from all countries.

There were 6,782 persons serving overseas as Roman Catholic missionaries in 1960, representing an increase of 10 per cent over 1958. Among these, 2,405 were in Latin America, 2,070 in Asia, and 781 in Africa. The missionaries in 1960 included 3,020 priests, 575 brothers, 170 scholastics, and 128 lay persons; about one-third of them had originally come from five large archdioceses: Boston, Brooklyn, New York, Philadelphia, and Chicago. Although American Roman Catholics constitute only 4 per cent of the total of Catholic missionaries, the United States is the major source of financial support for this world-wide service.

(NOTE: Data: for Protestants have been supplied by the Missionary Research Library, New York; for Roman Catholics, by the Mission Secretariat, Washington, D.C.)

Religions of Canada. "What is your religion?" was one of the questions asked in the 1961 Census of Canada. (A report of findings was issued by the Dominion Bureau of Statistics, Ottawa, as No. AP-8, Catalogue No. 92-522—price, 25¢.) In this study, enumerators were instructed to "inquire more fully" if such general terms as "Christian," "Protestant," or "believer" were given in reply. Such replies were accepted if a specific religious denomination could not be ascertained, but if a person stated that he had no religion, the entry "none" was recorded.

The published Census figures as published (which should not be confused with reports of membership issued by the various denominations) are as follows:

Anglican Church of Canada	2,409,068
Baptist	593,553
Greek Orthodox	239,766
Jews	254,368
Lutheran	662,744
Mennonite	152,452
Pentecostal	143,877
Presbyterian	818,558
Roman Catholic	8,342,826
Ukrainian (Greek Catholic)	189,653
United Church of Canada	3,664,008
Other	767,374
Total	18,238,247

World Constituents of Anglican and the Larger Protestant Groups. The data for Anglican and the large Protestant groups (compiled from the *World Christian Handbook,* London, 1962 and from later estimates made by the larger Protestant and the Anglican bodies throughout the world) are as follows:

Lutheran	72,500,000
Presbyterian and Reformed	45,000,000
Baptist	50,000,000
Methodist	40,000,000
Anglicans	40,000,000
Congregational	5,000,000
Other	7,500,000
Total	260,000,000

World Religions: Estimates of Adherents. Recent Data for membership in the principal world religions are as follows:

Buddhist	160,000,000
Christian, Total	965,000,000
(Eastern Orthodox)	135,000,000
(Protesant and Anglican)	260,000,000
(Roman Catholic)	570,000,000
Confucian	300,000,000
Hindu	390,000,000
Jewish	14,000,000
Muslim	445,000,000
Shinto	50,000,000
Taoist	50,000,000
Zoroastrian	150,000

NOTE: The more nearly global the figure, the greater the difficulty of estimating it. In the Orient, many adhere to two religions: for example, they may be both Buddhists and Confucians, or Confucians and Taoist, or Shintoists and Buddhists. The above estimates are based on several sources: revisions of estimates in the author's *World Religions* (1957); the *National Catholic Almanac* (1963); and Charles S. Braden's estimate in the *Britannica Book of the Year, 1964*. (The most recent global figures obtainable were for the year 1962.)

INDEX